Also by MARIAN BURROS

Pure & Simple

by MARIAN BURROS and LOIS LEVINE

The Elegant but Easy Cookbook
Come for Cocktails, Stay for Supper
Freeze with Ease
Second Helpings

by LOIS LEVINE

The Kids in the Kitchen Cookbook

THE
SUMMERTIME
COOKBOOK

by MARIAN BURROS and LOIS LEVINE

Illustrations by Rosalie Petrash Schmidt

The Summertime Cookbook

Elegant but Easy Dining– Indoors and Out

COLLIER BOOKS
A Division of Macmillan Publishing Co., Inc.
New York

COLLIER MACMILLAN PUBLISHERS
London

Macmillan Publishing Co., Inc.
866 Third Avenue, New York, N.Y. 10022
Collier Macmillan Canada, Ltd.

Library of Congress Cataloging in Publication Data
Burros, Marian Fox.
    The summertime cookbook.
    Includes index.
    1. Picnicking.   2. Outdoor cookery.   I. Levine,
Lois, joint author.   II. Title.
TX823.B88   1980   641.5   79-20799
ISBN 0-02-011190-8

First Collier Books Edition 1980

10   9   8   7   6   5   4   3   2

The Summertime Cookbook was originally published in a hardcover edition by Macmillan Publishing Co., Inc.

Printed in the United States of America

To our husbands,
Donald and Paul

Contents

Introduction:
Summertime and the Cookin' Is Easy   1

Summertime Menus   7

ᵃᵍ

Hot Hors d'Oeuvres   19

ᵃᵍ

Cold Hors d'Oeuvres   28

ᵃᵍ

Soups   54

ᵃᵍ

Meat Dishes   63

ᵃᵍ

Poultry Dishes   84

ᵃᵍ

Seafood Dishes   97

ᵃᵍ

Vegetables   106

Potato, Noodle, and Rice Dishes   114

❧

Salads and Cold Vegetables   125

❧

Breads   152

❧

Cakes and Pies   163

❧

Cookies and Small Cakes   184

❧

Cold Desserts   196

❧

Drinks   213

❧

Index   217

THE
SUMMERTIME
COOKBOOK

Introduction:
Summertime and
the Cookin' Is Easy

One never need picnic or dine alfresco to enjoy the recipes in this book. Anything that tastes good outside will taste almost as good indoors.

But whether you are a lover of creature comforts who won't leave the confines of a climate-controlled house, or a worshipper of the sun, countryside, and backyard flower garden, cooking in the summer should be different in at least two respects from any other time of year.

The glorious bounty of fruits and vegetables ought to be utilized whenever possible: Not only because it tastes so much better than last winter's apples or artichokes but also because seasonal foods are less expensive.

For some, an even more important reason is the heat and humidity. When it's ninety degrees in the shade, who needs oven roasts and cauldrons of steaming chowder in a kitchen ten degrees hotter than anywhere else?

Cooking in the cool of the early morning or late evening is a simple solution to hot weather. But if the kitchen has to be heated up, then the best place to eat is outside.

For some, picnics are a way of life in warm weather either for their own sakes or as a delightful and convenient way to eat before some other event like an outdoor concert or summer theater.

The occasion dictates the picnic site, food, and equipment. The occasion for patio dining also dictates the simplicity or elaborateness of the food and setting.

For many, the best alfresco dining is the one with the least amount of work. But they, no doubt, feel the same about eating indoors. Even for them, there is a picnic in this book. (Everything comes from the store.)

Many hostesses take the occasion of an unusual setting to create an elaborate menu in the manner of the English, who probably give better picnics than anyone else in the world. They think nothing of bringing along their best china, silver, and damask and literally re-creating an elaborate dining room setting in some green and wooded spot or by the cool waters of a babbling brook. It's fun and it's glamorous. And it is just as much work as a fancy dinner at home.

On the other hand, the relaxation of a casual picnic in the country—where the most comfortable clothes can be worn; the children are free to roam; and the paper napkins and plates can be tossed away—is what appeals to many people.

In each instance adequate planning is the key to success. You can't return to the kitchen for the forgotten bottle opener; the kitchen may be fifteen miles away. So a check list is essential.

ABSOLUTE NECESSITIES

If you picnic often, it is just as well to keep a container filled with these items. Almost every picnic requires most of them:

salt and pepper
bug repellant
wash-and-dry towels
can and bottle openers
napkins
food nets

ALMOST ABSOLUTE NECESSITIES

The following items are needed more often than not:

plates and cups
forks, spoons, and knives
tablecloth (cloth or heavy plastic or
  tatami matting) with anchors to fight the breezes
wide-mouth insulated containers for carrying ice
disposable foil grills
beach chairs

NOT NECESSITIES BUT A GREAT HELP

To picnic simply and properly the following items are helpful:
Insulated containers, which today are so inexpensive that one can afford several varieties.

The styrofoam carriers, also very cheap, will hold the food that should be kept cold or hot.

Insulated bottles and jars will hold the liquids.

Ice packs that are frozen ahead and reusable keep anything cold for a short period of time.

In a pinch, many thicknesses of newspaper are good insulators.

And when price is no object:

There is a porcelain-finished aluminum saucepan that comes in its own foam-plastic casing to keep casseroles hot or salads cold for as long as twelve hours. The same type of container also comes as a three-quart, covered, stainless mixing bowl.

There is a plastic-lined carrier that keeps food cold with a special lid. The lid, which contains water in a sealed section, is frozen before the jar is filled; the contents are kept chilled for hours. It's perfect for carrying the worrisome potato salad.

For picnics close to home, plastic refrigerator containers are handy. For extra protection the food can be put in a small jar and that jar set into a larger one filled with ice cubes. The snap top lids will keep the melting ice from diluting the food.

PREVENTING SPOILAGE

It is absolutely essential to keep foods from spoiling, unless you want your picnic to end up with a trek to the hospital. Holding perishables at room temperature is dangerous to health. The trick is to keep hot foods hot and cold foods cold.

Some items can be carried frozen to the picnic site and will thaw on the way.

Some dishes can be heated at home; carried hot and if further reheating is required, this can be done on top of a portable grill or over an alcohol burner.

HELPFUL HINTS

Little tricks learned along the way may save you much time and energy:

Deviled eggs, synonymous with picnics, can be carried more easily in an egg carton.

Bar cookies and some cakes ride well in their original baking pans.

When packing the picnic basket, wrap individual place settings of flatware in a napkin or two and secure, if desired, with a colorful pipe cleaner.

Pack the basket in reverse order of unloading, that is, the tablecloth should be on top.

Keep the carriers of hot and cold food out of direct sunlight.

Items such as smoked meats, cold fried chicken, breads, and unfilled pastries are less susceptible to spoilage and may be carried without benefit of insulating container.

PATIO PARTYING

Eating in the backyard (the word is interchangeable with patio and garden, depending on what it looks like and what kind of party you are throwing) isn't very different from eating in your dining room. But a lot of footsteps can be eliminated with some careful planning.

If you have an electric outlet outside, an electric warming tray will keep foods hot. Failing that, chafing dishes, candle warmers, and alcohol burners will do about the same. Ditto the grill.

Buffet servers are available with room for ice cubes below the food to keep the cold foods from wilting.

Outdoor ashtrays can be made easily by filling large clay flowerpots with sand and inserting a large, frankly fake blossom.

Outdoor lighting, if not possible electrically, is easily achieved with candles, preferably the bug-repellant variety and/or torches that burn bug-repellant fuel.

Outdoor cooking usually takes place on a grill. And if you are contemplating the purchase of one, consider the kind with a cover. It is far more versatile and gives the cook greater flexibility in temperature range.

But topless or not, if the grill is not to be transported, it should be as heavy as possible for longer wear. And the larger the better, as long as it can be rolled from place to place. Look for the rustproof variety with adjustable cooking surface, dampers, and easy access to the cinders.

An adjustable electric spit is great if you do that kind of rotisserie cooking. So is a wooden cutting surface.

For carrying around, a lightweight folding grill is desirable; it, too, should have an adjustable cooking surface.

Gas grills eliminate the fire maker and perhaps, for some, most of the fun. They are heated either by ceramic briquettes below the food or infra-red burners above it. Many feel the food doesn't have the same flavor as charcoal cooking.

Hibachis are attractive for small scale barbecuing.

Smokers are especially designed for smoking foods; but some covered grills can be adapted to the same purpose.

Your pocketbook and your interest in outdoor cooking must be your guide.

TO COOK IT INSIDE

Obviously some recipes for picnic dishes must be the pre-pared-ahead kind. But, as a matter of fact, except for the meats cooked on the grill, most of the recipes in the book fall into that category. It's the kind of cooking we like best and the kind we always have advocated, winter or summer.

The same key system—an asterisk * for freezable dishes and a number sign # (with 1, 2, or 3 beside it for number of days) for those that can be prepared ahead and refrigerated before serving—is used in this book as it was in our previous ones.

After all, if it rains, the whole delicious meal can be moved right indoors, and the cook can still be relaxed and comfortable with her guests.

COOK'S NOTES:

During the summer fresh herbs are more readily available and those who cultivate them may want to substitute them for the dried. The rule of thumb is: three to one. Use 3 teaspoons (1 tablespoon) fresh herbs for every teaspoon of dried herbs.

In trying to be as specific as possible, can sizes are given in ounces. Frequently the specific size is not available where you shop. For most recipes there is no problem about substituting a 6-ounce can for a 5¾-ounce can or a 6½-ounce can for a 7-ounce can. Within an ounce, substitutions are perfectly all right and will not affect the recipe.

Summertime
Menus

Patio *Knives, Forks, and Dessert Spoons*
Italian Olive Spread
Roast Beef Californian
Sea Breeze Spinach Mold
Hot Rolls
Burgundy or Bordeaux
Fruit with Cream

Patio *Forks and Dessert Forks*
Spiked Melon Balls
Picadinho
Rice (6 cups cooked)
Mixed Bag Salad
Burgundy
Sherley's Mocha Ice Box Cake

Patio *Knives, Forks, and Dessert Spoons*
Deviled Meat Balls
Wente Chicken
Broiled Seasoned Tomatoes
Chick Pea Salad
Dry White Wine
Cold Peach Soufflé

Cookout   *Knives and Forks*
Camembert Nut Sandwiches
Michael's Grilled Steak
Sunshine Pasta
Tomato Cheese Salad
French Rolls
Burgundy
Orange Marmalade Bars

Cookout   *Knives and Forks*
Lulu Paste
Grilled Lime Chicken
Three Bean Salad
Cheese Ring Loaf
Beer
Oatmeal Wafers

Brunch (at home or away)   *Knives and Forks*
Bloody Marys and Screwdrivers
Melon Wedges
Pâté Quiche
Farmhouse Bread
Bagels, Cream Cheese, and Smoked Salmon
Chocolate Nut Loaf
Grapes and Tomme de Savoie, Brie, and Cheddar Cheeses

Mexican Patio Fiesta   *Knives, Forks, and Dessert Spoons*
Mock Pâté*
Guacamole with Tortillas or Corn Chips
Huachinango Veracruzano (Red Snapper)
Boiled Potatoes
Green Salad with Vinaigrette Dressing
Beer
Caramel Flan

* French food is very popular in Mexico in the better restaurants. Pâté
is often on the menu.

Patio Buffet   *Knives and Forks*
Olive Tarts
Stuffed Lychees
Curried Chicken and Broccoli
Elkridge Tomatoes
Hot Buttery Rolls
Beer
Pecan Tarts

Patio   *Knives and Forks*
Crabmeat Surprise
Ernie's Chicken Provençal
Rice
Cucumber Mousse
White Wine
Praline Cake

Rehoboth Patio Special   *Knives, Forks, and Dessert Forks*
Ham and Pineapple Puffs
Maryland Crabcakes
Zucchini Salad
Onion Cheese Bread
Beer
Macadamia Nut Ice Box Cake

Patio   *Forks only*
Chili Cheese Roll
Farmer in the Dell
Chinese Noodles or Rice
Honey Lime Salad
Beer or White Wine
Meringue Cookies

Curry Cookout   *Forks and Dessert Spoons*
Parmesan Sticks
Lamb Curry
"Eleven Boy" Condiments
Rice
Beer
Blossie's Special or Peaches or Nectarines with Sour Cream

Backyard Barbecue   *Knives and Forks*
Chinese Chicken Wings
Southwestern Lamb
Baked Potatoes Florentine
Guacamole Salad
Rosé Wine
Anita's Coffeecake

Barbecue   *Knives, Forks, and Dessert Forks*
Broccoli Flowers
Barbecued Beef Roast
Confetti Rice
Egg and Avocado Salad
Red Wine
Italian Cheese Pie

Patio Luncheon   *Forks and Dessert Spoons*
Shangri La Dip
Armenian Salad
Orange Pecan Bread
Jellied Melon
Rosé Wine
Filled Marzipan Cookies

Barbecue   *Knives, Forks, and Dessert Forks*
Bacon Wrapped Shrimp
Calypso Chicken Barbecue
Almond Crunch Rice
Strawberry Cranberry Mold
Beer
Ginger Peachy Flan

Sunday Supper on Patio   *Forks and Dessert Spoons*
Appetizer Cheese Cake
Noodles Italienne
Red Cabbage Filled with Cole Slaw
Betsy's Herb Bread
White Wine
Raspberry Macaroon Mousse

Elegant Barbecue   *Knives, Forks, and Dessert Forks*
Chicken Pâté Loaf (cold)
Oriental Salmon Steaks
Tene's Noodle Pudding
Orange and Blue Cheese Salad
Rosé Wine
Lemon Cream Torte

One for the Kids-Cookout   *Forks only*
Crab Caper Dip
Hamburgers Diable
Potatoes in Armor
Guacamole Tomatoes
Beer and Soda
Molasses Chewies

Family Reunion Barbecue   *Forks and Dessert Forks*
Chutnut Roll
Honey Glazed Spareribs
Hot Potato Salad
Lemon Zucchini
Beer
Blueberry Pie with Orange Nut Crust

Patio Party for 8   *Knives, Forks, and Dessert Spoons*
Shrimp Italiano
Grilled Sirloin
Green Onion Pie
Cole Slaw Salad
Red Wine or Beer
Marquise de Chocolat

International Barbecue   *Knives, Forks, and Dessert Forks*
Polynesian Dip
South African Shish Kebob
Curried Rice
Roman Salad
Beer
Strawberry Nut Tart

Backyard Barbecue   *Knives, Forks, and Dessert Forks*
Caviar Frosted Cheese Mold
London Broil Béarnaise
Individual Yorkshire Puddings
Western Toss
Red Wine
Rhubarb and Strawberry Pie

Patio Dinner   *Forks and Dessert Spoons*
Melon and Avocado with Prosciutto
Cold Salmon—Sauce Verte
Spiced Apricot Mold
Sangria or White Wine
Coffee Parfait

Barbecue Feast   *Knives, Forks, and Dessert Spoons*
Gazpacho
Barbecued Lamb with Plum Sauce
Zucchini with Sour Cream
Roasted Corn on the Cob
Beer or Rosé Wine
Pêches Françaises

PICNIC AWAY

Before the Concert   *Soup Spoons, Forks, Knives, and*
                                             Dessert Forks
Empanadas
Cold Spinach Soup
Chicken in Tuna Sauce with Cherry Tomatoes on Rice Bed
White Wine
Peachy Cocoa Torte

Before the Summer Theater   *Knives and Forks*
Nippy Four Cheese Ball
Meat Loaf Lollipops
Molded Potato Salad
Cherry Tomatoes
French Bread and Brie
Red Bordeaux
Lemon Curd Miniature Tarts

Late Summer Mountain Lunch   *Soup Spoons only*
Beef and Barley Soup
Cheese Buttermilk Bread
Beer
Fruit
Applesauce Shortcake Squares

Barge Picnic   *Forks only*
Chili Dip
Nancy's Chicken and Rice Salad
Dilly Beans
Biscuits
Beer
Hello Dollys

Sailing Picnic   *Forks and Soup Spoons*
Onion Pie
Tomato Lime Soup
Pic-l-nic Beef Roll on Rolls
Vegetable Antipasto
Burgundy
Delice Cheese Bars

On the Beach   *Spoons only*
Tom Thumbs
Rehoboth Chowder
Poor Boy and Pain Bagnat Sandwiches (tuna and salami)
Fruits—Watermelon, Honeydew, and Cantaloupe Wedges;
    Plums, Peaches, Strawberries
Beer
Dundee Cake

Picnic in the Park *Forks and Dessert Forks*
Double Cheese Roll
Baked Corned Beef
Marinated Beans
Poppy Seed Rolls
Beer
Tipsy Delight

Fête Champêtre *Soup Spoons, Knives, and Forks*
Pâté en Terrine
Iced Curry Soup
Saumon en Croute with Lemon Mayonnaise
Macaroni Picnic Bowl
White Wine
Three D Brownies

On the Road *Forks*
Bloody Marys
Stuffed Eggs
Picnic Fried Chicken
Celery with Cheese Filling
Beaten Biscuits
Camembert and Sour Dough French Bread
Glazed Chocolate Chip Cake

Tailgating—Night Game *Forks only*
Pimiento Cheese Spread
Chili Con Sausage
Bea's Ratatouille
Rolls
Beer
Devil's Food Cake

Picnic to Carry Anywhere   *Forks only*
Eggplant Caviar
Norwegian Meat Pie
Mixed Vegetable Salad
Herb Bread
Red Bordeaux
Grape Bavarian

Store-bought Picnic
2 Cheese Spreads—blue and Cheddar
1 pint Bean Salad
1 pint Cold Vegetable Salad
4 to 6 slices Pâté
8 slices German Salami
4 Beef Sticks
4 to 6 slices Teawurst or Liverwurst
8 slices Corned Beef
Rye Bread
Crackers
Mustard
Red Wine
Cookies
Fruit
(Sandwich fillings: corned beef and blue cheese spread: salami
and Cheddar cheese spread)

Sunday School Picnic   *Knives and Forks*
Zippy Avocado Dip
Stuffed Mushroom Caps
Sesame Chicken
Vegetable Salad
Beer and Soda
Pat's Chocoroon Cupcakes

French Countryside   *Soup Spoons and Forks*
Easy Vichyssoise
Salade Niçoise
French Bread
White Wine
Apricot Marzipan Tart

Greek Picnic   *Forks and Dessert Forks*
Black Olives with Green Butter
Moussaka à la Grecque
Greek Salad
Syrian or Arabic Bread
Red Wine or Retsina
Kataifi

Picnic Luncheon at Stratford   *Soup Spoons and Forks*
Cheese Taster's Choice
Jiffy Gazpacho
Chicken Gauguin
Orange Cranberry Muffins
White Wine or Sangria
Brownie Torte

By the Side of a Stream   *Forks and Dessert Spoons*
Potted Cheddar
Chicken Pineapple Salad
Broccoli Vinaigrette
Onion Herb Ring
White Wine
Strawberries Romanoff

Picnic Luncheon   *Soup Spoons and Forks*
Chilled Shrimp Bisque
Danish Loaf
Avocado and Melon Salad
Sangria
Spicy Sponge Cake

Picnic Lunch   *Soup Spoons, Forks, and Dessert Forks*
Moon Cheese
Cucumber Soup
Lobster Luncheon Salad
Herb Bread Sticks
White Wine
Cold Rhubarb Soufflé

Hot Hors D'Oeuvres

BACON WRAPPED SHRIMP

makes 4 dozen

Combine and refrigerate for dip

- 2 hard-cooked eggs, finely chopped
- ¾ cup mayonnaise
- 6 tablespoons finely chopped sweet pickle
- 2 tablespoons finely chopped pimiento-stuffed olives
- 1 tablespoon grated onion
- 1 tablespoon chili powder

Cook as directed, then chill

1 pound frozen, peeled shrimp (about 4 dozen)

Combine and heat in saucepan

½ cup butter
1½ teaspoons chili powder
1 clove garlic, crushed

Wrap around each shrimp and secure with toothpick

¼ slice partially cooked bacon (use 1 pound very thin)

Up to this point, preparation can be done a day ahead. To serve, return shrimp to room temperature and arrange on broiler rack. Broil 3 inches from heat, brushing with melted butter mixture. Broil and turn until bacon is crisp. Serve hot shrimp with cold dip.

CHINESE CHICKEN WINGS   *makes about 30*

* #1
Cut off and discard tips from

3 pounds chicken wings

Cut each remaining wing into two parts. Sprinkle with

salt
pepper
2 tablespoons vegetable oil

Combine and pour over wings

  1 cup honey
  ½ cup soy sauce
  1 clove garlic, mashed
  2 tablespoons catsup

Bake in shallow 10-by-15-pan for 50 minutes at 375°. Refrigerate or freeze. When ready to serve, reheat on top of grill, wrapped in foil, for 10 minutes.

DEVILED MEAT BALLS   *makes about 2 dozen*

* #2

Crumble

  2 ounces Roquefort cheese

Blend in

  ¼ cup mayonnaise
  1 tablespoon Worcestershire sauce
  1 teaspoon prepared mustard

Crush

  2 cups cornflakes

Combine with first mixture. Add

  ½ cup milk
  1 egg, slightly beaten
  1 pound ground beef
  ½ teaspoon salt
  ⅛ teaspoon pepper

Form into small balls about 1 inch in diameter. Refrigerate or freeze. To serve, bring to room temperature and broil or pan fry to desired doneness.

EMPANADAS
makes 32 small; 16 large

*#1

Made with refrigerator crescent roll dough, this may not be authentic Spanish cuisine, but it's much easier and very good.

Brown

    ¾ pound ground chuck

Add and brown

    ¾ cup chopped onion

Stir in

    ¾ cup canned tomatoes, drained
  1¼ teaspoons salt
    ¼ teaspoon dried oregano
    ¼ teaspoon hot pepper sauce
    ½ cup chopped black olives
    2 hard-cooked eggs, chopped
    4 tablespoons raisins

Cook for several minutes, until ingredients are well blended. Pour off all excess liquid and cool.

Open

2 (8-ounce) cans refrigerator crescent rolls

Flatten each triangle of dough with palm of hand. (For small empanadas, cut triangles in half.) Place a teaspoon of filling in center of small empanadas; about 1 tablespoon in large. Use as much filling as possible in each piece. Close up by folding in sides and sealing edges by pressing with fork tines. Bake at 375° for 20 to 30 minutes, depending on size. Freeze if desired. After returning to room temperature, reheat in oven just enough to warm through, about 8 minutes at 350°.

HAM PINEAPPLE PUFFS

makes 32

✿

Heat

    3 tablespoons butter
    ½ to ¾ teaspoon curry powder

Add to butter and cook until vegetables are softened

    3 tablespoons finely chopped green onion
    ⅓ cup finely chopped celery
    1½ cups finely chopped cooked ham

Remove from heat and stir in

    a heaping ⅛ teaspoon dry mustard
    4½ tablespoons mayonnaise
    1 (15-ounce) can crushed pineapple, drained

Cool and pour off any excess liquid.
Open and separate into triangles

2 (8-ounce) cans refrigerator crescent rolls

Roll out each triangle on lightly floured board and cut into 2 triangles. Place a teaspoon of filling in center of triangle and bring sides in together as if to form a pouch, twisting loose ends. Cut off excess dough, being sure the twist is securely fastened. Bake at 375° for 20 minutes or until golden brown. Serve warm. Or bake at 375° for 10 minutes; cool and freeze. To serve, return to room temperature and bake at 375° for about 10 minutes, until golden brown.

OLIVE TARTS
makes 3½ dozen

❋

Mix well

2 cups grated sharp Cheddar cheese
½ cup butter, softened

Stir in

1 cup sifted flour
½ teaspoon salt
1 teaspoon paprika
⅛ to ¼ teaspoon cayenne pepper

Mix well into smooth dough. Take a small ball of dough and flatten with hand. Wrap it around well-drained olive from

1 (10-ounce) jar medium to small, pimiento-stuffed green olives

Make a ball around the olive. Depending on size olives used, there may be some left over. Freeze until ready to serve. Bake at 400° for 12 to 15 minutes directly from freezer. Serve warm or at room temperature.

PÂTÉ QUICHE

serves 6

*#1
Bake at 375° for 5 minutes

   1 (9-inch) pie shell

Cool and spread the bottom of the shell with contents of

   1 (2¾-ounce) can liver pâté

Top with

   1 cup thinly sliced Swiss cheese

Beat together

      4 eggs
   1¼ cups heavy cream

Add

   ½ teaspoon salt
   dash of cayenne pepper
   ¼ teaspoon nutmeg
   ⅓ cup chopped onion

Freeze or refrigerate if desired. To bake, return to room temperature and bake at 350° for about 40 to 45 minutes, or until knife inserted 1 inch from edge comes out clean. Serve warm, not hot.

SWISS ONION PIE
serves 6 to 8

#1
Cook until tender and translucent

>   **3 cups thinly sliced, sweet Spanish onions**

in

>   **3 tablespoons butter**

Cool. Fry until not quite done

>   **6 slices bacon**

Drain on paper toweling. Cut in 1-inch lengths.
With fork whip until blended

>   **2 eggs**

Combine and mix until smooth

>   **1 tablespoon flour**
>   **2 tablespoons milk**

Add to eggs along with

     1½ cups sour cream
      6 tablespoons milk
     ½ teaspoon salt
     half the bacon

Spoon the onion into a

9-inch unbaked pastry shell, chilled

Pour custard mixture over onions. Top with remaining bacon. Bake at 400° about 35 to 40 minutes, until custard is firm. Serve at room temperature.

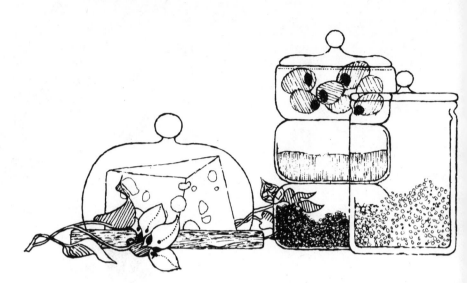

Cold Hors D'Oeuvres

APPETIZER CHEESE CAKE

#1

Brush bottom and sides of 9-inch spring form pan with

melted butter

Crumble in blender

1 **(6-ounce) box cheese crackers**

Reserving half of crumbs for top, sprinkle rest on bottom of spring form. Combine in blender until finely chopped

   2 cups sour cream
   ½ cup pimiento-stuffed green olives
   1 medium green pepper, seeded and cut up
   1 small onion, quartered
   2 tablespoons lemon juice
   1 teaspoon salt
   1 teaspoon Worcestershire sauce
   1 large stalk celery, cut in pieces
   2 tablespoons unflavored gelatin

Spread carefully over crumb base. Scatter remaining crumbs on top. Cover and refrigerate at least 24 hours. Remove sides of pan. Garnish with

   ripe olives and pimiento strips

Serve on slices of

   party rye or pumpernickel

BLACK OLIVES WITH
GREEN BUTTER

#3
Cream together

   3 tablespoons butter
   1 teaspoon minced fresh parsley
   1 shallot or 1 green onion, minced
   ½ teaspoon vinegar

   2 teaspoons anchovy paste
   1 teaspoon minced capers
   2 teaspoons minced sweet pickles
  ½ teaspoon salt
  ¼ teaspoon paprika

Use to stuff

  40 large, pitted black olives

CAMEMBERT NUT SANDWICHES

*#3

Cream until light and fluffy

  ¼ cup softened butter

Blend in

  ¼ cup finely chopped pecans
     a few drops of hot pepper sauce
   1 tablespoon lemon juice

Cut in half, horizontally

   1 (8-ounce) wheel Camembert cheese

Do this while it is chilled for ease in cutting. Spread butter mixture between halves to make a sandwich. Chill until filling is firm; freeze if desired.

Before serving, allow to stand at room temperature for 1½ hours, if it was refrigerated, to get full flavor. If frozen, it will take longer.

Serve with

   melba toast or mild crackers

CAVIAR FROSTED CHEESE MOLD

#1
Blend in blender until smooth

    1 cup sour cream
    1 cup creamed cottage cheese
    1 clove garlic, crushed
    1 teaspoon Worcestershire sauce
    1 teaspoon salt
    ¼ teaspoon pepper
    ½ teaspoon soy sauce
    a few drops of hot pepper sauce

Soften

    1 tablespoon unflavored gelatin

in

    ¼ cup dry sherry

Then place over hot water until gelatin dissolves. Add to cream cheese mixture and whip until light. Pour into lightly greased 1-pint mold. Chill at least 24 hours before serving. Unmold onto platter. Mix together

    4 ounces red caviar

with

    juice of ½ lemon

Frost cheese mold with caviar. Serve with

    unsalted crackers or melba rounds

CELERY WITH CHEESE FILLING *about 25 2-inch pieces*

#1
Clean

    celery stalks

Combine and mix thoroughly

    4 **ounces cream cheese**
    2 **tablespoons sour cream**
    1 **tablespoon butter**
  1½ **teaspoons minced capers**
   ¼ **teaspoon anchovy paste**
   ¼ **teaspoon minced onion**
   ¼ **teaspoon dry mustard**
   ¼ **teaspoon paprika**

Fill the celery stalks with this mixture and cut into 2-inch pieces.
Cover well and refrigerate.

CHEESE TASTER'S CHOICE

*#3
Combine and mix until well blended

    8 **ounces cream cheese**
   ¼ **cup milk**
    2 **cups (8 ounces) shredded sharp Cheddar cheese**

Divide cheese mixture into three equal parts, about ⅔ cup each. To one portion add

> 2 slices crisply cooked bacon, crumbled
> 2 tablespoons chopped green onion

To second portion add

> ¼ cup crushed pineapple, drained
> 1 tablespoon blue cheese
> ½ teaspoon finely chopped candied ginger

To remaining portion add

> ¼ cup salted peanuts, chopped
> 1 tablespoon chopped pimiento

Place each variety in an individual jar. Refrigerate or freeze. Let guests spread their own choice on crackers.

CHICKEN PÂTÉ LOAF

#1
Very rich, very elegant.

Boil until tender, then dice

> 1 whole chicken breast, boned and skinned

Melt in a skillet

> 2 tablespoons butter

Brown in butter and cook quickly for 2 minutes

½ pound chicken livers

Add and cook for 2 minutes more

2 shallots, chopped
½ pound mushrooms, sliced

Pour over livers

¼ cup dry sherry

Add and simmer for 1 minute

1 cup chicken broth
½ teaspoon salt
¼ teaspoon pepper

Strain broth and measure out 1½ cups liquid. If not enough liquid, add a little more chicken broth. Place in blender

1 envelope unflavored gelatin
¼ cup water

Heat ¾ cup reserved broth to boiling and mix with contents of blender. Add remaining broth. Add

¼ cup mayonnaise
½ cup heavy cream

Blend together by combining small amounts of chicken, livers, etc, with liquid until all is blended and smooth. Chill in 1-pint mold. Serve on

party rye

CHILI CHEESE ROLL

*#3
Melt over boiling water

   1 **pound Cheddar cheese**
   1 **pound cream cheese**
   1 **pound garlic-flavored snappy cheese roll***

Add

   3 **tablespoons prepared mustard**
   2 **hot chili peppers, minced**
   3 **tablespoons Worcestershire sauce**
   3 **cloves garlic, pressed**

Mix well and simmer 20 to 30 minutes; chill and then divide
into six parts. Form each part into a roll with diameter about
1½ inches. Sprinkle

   chili powder

generously on a square of foil and roll cheese in it to coat completely. Wrap in foil and twist ends. Refrigerate or freeze, if
desired. Serve at room temperature with crackers. This cheese
mixture can also be reheated and served hot as a dip.

   * Or use soft, processed cheese and add another clove garlic.

CHILI DIP

#3
Brown

    2 **pounds ground chuck**

Add and sauté until tender

    3 **medium onions, chopped**
    1 **green pepper, chopped**

Add

    2 **tablespoons chili powder**
    1 **can condensed tomato soup**
    1 **(8-ounce) can tomato sauce**
    1 **(6-ounce) can tomato paste**

Cook for 10 minutes. Then add

    1 **pound processed, soft American cheese**

Cook until cheese melts. Serve dip hot surrounded by

    corn chips

Refrigerate or freeze, if desired. To serve, return to room temperature and heat through.

CHUTNUT ROLL

*#3
Mix together

>   ¼ pound blue cheese
>   ½ pound cream cheese
>   ¼ cup chopped chutney

Form into large roll and roll this in

>   ½ cup chopped toasted almonds

Chill thoroughly or freeze. Defrost if frozen and serve with

crackers

CRAB CAPER DIP

#2
Combine and chill thoroughly

>   1 cup sour cream
>   ¼ cup mayonnaise
>   ½ pound crabmeat
>   1 tablespoon capers
>   1 tablespoon grated onion
>   1 tablespoon lemon juice
>   1 clove garlic, mashed
>   salt and pepper to taste

Serve with

potato chips

CRABMEAT SURPRISE

#1
Pick over for cartilage and shells

lump crabmeat

Cut into thin strips

thinly sliced prosciutto ham

Fasten a strip of ham around a large lump of crabmeat. Combine according to taste and strength desired

mayonnaise
Dijon mustard
chopped fresh chives

Serve the sauce as a dip for the crabmeat wrapped in prosciutto. Allow 3 to 4 per person.

DOUBLE CHEESE ROLL

#3
Cook until crisp

3 or 4 strips bacon

Drain and crumble.

Combine

>   **8 ounces shredded Cheddar cheese**
>   **½ cup crumbled blue cheese**

Mix together until well blended. Shape into roll. Roll in crumbled bacon and refrigerate.
Wrap well in foil. Serve with

>   **crackers**

EGGPLANT CAVIAR

*#3
A Russian hors d'oeuvre, enjoyed by anyone who likes good food.

Puncture with a fork

>   **3 pounds eggplant**

Bake them on cookie sheets for 1½ hours at 400°. Remove skins and cool. Cut eggplants in half. Chop pulp. Cover the bottom of large frying pan with

>   **oil**

Sauté

>   **¾ pound onions, finely chopped**

in hot oil until golden. Add

    3 carrots, finely grated
    ½ green pepper, finely grated

Simmer 10 minutes. Add eggplant along with

    ½ (6-ounce) can tomato paste
    ½ (8-ounce) can tomato sauce
    1 tablespoon vinegar
    juice of ¼ lemon
    salt and pepper to taste

Mix thoroughly. Cover and cook over low heat 45 minutes, stirring occasionally. Add

    2 tablespoons dry red wine

Cook 15 minutes longer. Cool and refrigerate or freeze. To serve, defrost if necessary; serve chilled with

    party-size pumpernickel

ITALIAN OLIVE SPREAD

*#3
Combine

    6 ounces cream cheese, softened
    2 (4½-ounce) cans chopped black olives
    2 to 3 tablespoons spaghetti sauce mix

Refrigerate or freeze. To serve, return to room temperature and serve with

    crackers

LULU PASTE

#1
Where it got its name, no one knows! It is a piquant, creamy spread.

In top of double boiler combine

- 3 slightly beaten egg yolks
- 6 tablespoons sugar
- 6 tablespoons vinegar

Stir until mixture thickens. Pour mixture gradually over

- 12 ounces softened cream cheese

Stir until smooth. Add

- 1 small green pepper, chopped fine
- 1 medium onion, chopped fine

Refrigerate, if desired. Serve at room temperature with

crackers

MELON AND AVOCADO WITH PROSCIUTTO

#1
Peel and slice into bite-sized pieces

    1 large cantaloupe
    1 large avocado

Sprinkle with

    ¼ cup lemon juice

Marinate for 1 hour in

    1 cup French dressing

Using

    ½ pound sliced prosciutto

wrap each piece of fruit. Fasten with toothpicks.

MOCK PÂTÉ

#2
Blend together

    1 (4¾-ounce) can liver pâté
    4 ounces butter

Season to taste with a little

    salt and black pepper, freshly ground

Mix in

    3½ tablespoons dry vermouth

Place in crock or serving dish. Chill well and serve with

melba toast rounds

MOON CHEESE

*#3
It's green

Beat together

    8 ounces softened cream cheese
    2 tablespoons dried, crumbled sage
    2 tablespoons chopped green onion

Cover tightly. Refrigerate until firm or freeze. To serve, return to room temperature and shape into crescent "moon," smoothing top and sides with spatula. Lightly press sides and top with

    2 tablespoons poppy seeds

Chill until serving time. Serve with

    crackers

NIPPY FOUR CHEESE BALL   *makes 2 balls; 1 serves 8*

*#3
Bring to room temperature

    1 pound soft Cheddar
    1 pound cream cheese
    ¼ pound blue cheese
    ¼ pound smoked cheese

Mix together with

    1 tablespoon prepared mustard
    1 tablespoon onion salt
    ¼ teaspoon garlic salt
    4 tablespoons port wine

Add

    3 tablespoons horseradish sauce (see recipe below)

Mix well and chill. Then shape into 2 balls and refrigerate or freeze. (Refrigerate at least 1 day to meld flavors.) To serve, return to room temperature and coat with

    chopped pecans

Serve with

    party rye or pumpernickel

Horseradish Sauce:

Brown

    ¾ teaspoon chopped onion

in

    2 teaspoons butter

Add

    1½ teaspoons flour

Stir in

    ¼ cup milk or light cream

Cook, stirring until thickened. When thickened add

    1 tablespoon prepared white horseradish

PARMESAN STICKS

*#3
Cream

    ½ pound butter, softened
    1 cup finely chopped fresh parsley
    1 cup grated Parmesan cheese

Freeze

    1 loaf unsliced white bread

Remove crusts; slice very thinly while frozen. Spread butter mixture on frozen bread slices. Using scissors or knife, cut slices into 6 narrow strips each. Sprinkle with extra cheese. Place on ungreased cookie sheets and bake at 200° to 225° for 45 to 60 minutes, or until crisp and brown. Cool. Store in plastic bags. Freeze if desired. Serve at room temperature.

PÂTÉ EN TERRINE

makes about 3 cups

#3
Soak for 2 hours

  1 pound chicken livers

in

  ½ cup dry sherry
  ¼ teaspoon allspice

Drain, reserving livers. Discard marinade. Trim livers, leaving rounded whole pieces for center.
Grind liver trimmings and add to

  ½ cup ground bacon
  1 cup ground smoked ham

Mash to smooth paste and combine with

  2 egg yolks
  salt and freshly ground black pepper to taste
  ⅛ teaspoon allspice

Line the bottom of a small, greased terrine or loaf pan with half the paste. Arrange the whole livers carefully over the paste. Cover with remaining paste, pressing down to fill in all the spaces. Cover entire surface with

  4 slices fat bacon

Cover terrine or loaf pan with double thickness of heavy duty aluminum foil. Place in a pan containing water 1-inch deep.

Bake about 2 hours at 300° degrees. Cool. Remove bacon slices and store in refrigerator until serving time. Serve in terrine or unmold. Serve with

mildly flavored crackers

PIMIENTO CHEESE SPREAD *makes about 3 cups*

#3
Bring to room temperature

1 pound sharp Cheddar cheese, grated

Add

2 tablespoons green onions, chopped
1 (2-ounce) jar pimiento, finely chopped
¾ cup mayonnaise
¼ cup chopped pecans

Blend well until spreading consistency. Serve with

crackers

POLYNESIAN DIP

#2
Combine and mix well

  1 cup mayonnaise
  1 cup sour cream
  ¼ cup finely chopped onion
  ¼ cup minced parsley
  ¼ cup chopped water chestnuts
  1 or 2 tablespoons chopped candied ginger
  2 cloves garlic, minced
  1 tablespoon soy sauce
  dash of salt

Refrigerate at least 4 hours. When ready to serve top with

  additional candied ginger

Serve with

  sesame seed crackers

POTTED CHEDDAR

*#3
Blend together until smooth

  2 cups (8 ounces) shredded sharp Cheddar cheese
  2 tablespoons butter
  2 tablespoons Port wine
  ¼ teaspoon paprika

Refrigerate or freeze. Serve, cold but not frozen, with

  sesame seed crackers

SHANGRI LA DIP

#3
Combine and mix well

> 1 teaspoon curry powder
> ⅛ teaspoon salt
> ⅛ teaspoon garlic salt
> 1 teaspoon sugar
> 2 tablespoons chopped ripe olives
> 1 tablespoon prepared horseradish
> 1 cup sour cream

Serve with

> chips, crackers, or raw vegetables

SHRIMP ITALIANO

#1
Combine in saucepan and bring to a boil

> 2 cups chicken stock
> 2 tablespoons lemon juice
> 1 teaspoon salt

Add

> 1 pound peeled, uncooked shrimp

Bring to second boil. Remove from heat. Let stand one minute.
Drain shrimp and marinate for several hours in

1 bottle Italian dressing

When ready to serve, drain and impale shrimp on toothpicks, each with a

cherry tomato

SPIKED MELON BALLS   *makes 3 or 4 dozen*

#1
Cut into bite-sized wedges

2 cantaloupes or 1 large honeydew

Marinate overnight in refrigerator in

¼ to ⅓ cup orange liqueur

Drain and wrap around each melon wedge

a thin strip prosciutto ham

Fasten with pick and serve cold.

STUFFED EGGS   *makes 12 halves*

#1
Hard-cook

6 eggs

Shell eggs, cut in half and remove yolks. Mash yolks with

¼ teaspoon salt
⅛ teaspoon freshly ground black pepper
1 teaspoon Dijon mustard
½ teaspoon instant minced onion
⅛ teaspoon garlic powder
dash of cayenne pepper
1 teaspoon cider vinegar
2 tablespoons minced celery
3 tablespoons mayonnaise
½ teaspoon lemon juice

Fill egg whites with this mixture. Garnish with paprika and refrigerate.

STUFFED LYCHEES   *makes about 16*

#1
Drain

1 (20-ounce) can lychee nuts

Combine

3 ounces cream cheese
¼ cup finely chopped salted macadamia nuts or salted
pecans

Stuff the lychee nuts with cream mixture and refrigerate until serving time.

TOM THUMBS   *makes about 4 dozen*

#7
These keep very well for a week in a tightly sealed container.

Mix together thoroughly

> 8 ounces Cheddar cheese, grated
> ½ cup butter or margarine, softened

Mix in

> ⅓ cup sifted flour
> dash of cayenne pepper
> 3 cups ready-to-eat, high-protein cereal

Shape into rolls about 1 inch in diameter. Chill. Slice ¼-inch thick and bake at 325° for 12 to 15 minutes or until lightly browned around edges.

ZIPPY AVOCADO DIP

#1
Seed, peel, and mash

> 2 medium-sized, ripe avocados

Stir in

> 1 tablespoon canned green chiles, chopped
> 1 tablespoon onion juice

1 clove garlic, minced
2 teaspoons lemon juice
½ teaspoon salt

Blend well. Cover and chill. Serve with

   tortilla chips

Soups

BEEF AND BARLEY SOUP

makes about 2½ quarts

---

*#3
For a mountaintop picnic.

Drain, reserving juice,

2 cups canned tomatoes

Reserve tomatoes. Add enough water to juice to make 1 quart liquid. Place this in a large kettle with

¾ pound boneless chuck, cut into 1½-inch cubes
2¼ teaspoons salt
¼ teaspoon pepper
celery tops from ½ bunch
2 sprigs parsley

Cover and cook slowly for 1 hour. Add

¼ cup regular barley

Cook 1 hour longer. Remove and discard celery tops and parsley.
Add

1 cup tomato juice
reserved canned tomatoes (drained earlier)
½ (10-ounce) package frozen, cut green beans
½ cup coarsely chopped rutabaga
1½ cups coarsely chopped cabbage
½ cup sliced carrots
½ cup sliced celery
½ cup thinly sliced onion

Bring to a boil. Reduce heat and cook about 45 minutes. Cool
quickly and freeze, if desired, or refrigerate. To serve, reheat.

CHILLED SHRIMP BISQUE   *serves 8*

#1
Mix well together

2 cans frozen shrimp soup
2 soup cans buttermilk
2 cups peeled and chopped cucumber
2 teaspoons sugar
2 teaspoons prepared mustard

Chill. Garnish individual servings with

cucumber slices
dill weed

CUCUMBER SOUP
serves 8

#2
Heat in skillet

4 tablespoons butter

Sauté until wilted

½ cup green onions

Add and simmer 15 minutes

3 cups chopped, unpeeled cucumbers
¾ cup diced potatoes
4 cups chicken broth

During last 5 minutes add

1 cup watercress leaves

Add to taste

salt and pepper

Puree in blender, chill. When cooled, add

dash of hot pepper sauce
2 cups sour cream

Mix well and chill at least 2 hours or longer in nonmetallic container. To serve, garnish with

minced chives

EASY VICHYSSOISE   *serves 8*

#1
Combine in blender or mixer

> 3 (13-ounce) cans Vichyssoise
> 1½ cups sour cream
> 1 teaspoon grated onion

Beat until thoroughly combined. Chill at least 3 hours or until ready to serve. Serve in soup bowls or paper cups. Sprinkle top of each serving with

chopped chives

GAZPACHO   *serves 8*

#2
Blend on high speed in blender

> 2 large cucumbers, peeled and seeded
> 12 medium tomatoes, peeled
> 1 (4-ounce) jar red pimientos
> 4 teaspoons vinegar
> juice of 4 lemons

2 cloves garlic, chopped
½ teaspoon Worcestershire sauce
1 teaspoon sugar

Add and blend for 5 seconds

4 tablespoons olive oil

Add, but do not blend,

2 teaspoons chopped chives

Refrigerate thoroughly, and serve with following garnishes in separate bowls

garlic croutons
diced green pepper
diced black olives
diced cucumber

JIFFY GAZPACHO   *serves 8 to 10*

#1
Combine

2 cans condensed tomato soup
2 soup cans water
½ cup chopped onion
1 cup chopped green pepper
2 cups chopped cucumber
4 tablespoons olive oil
4 tablespoons wine vinegar
dash of hot pepper sauce

½ teaspoon salt
¼ teaspoon pepper

Blend small amounts at a time in blender for a few seconds. Refrigerate overnight. Serve in well-chilled bowls each topped with

lemon slices

ICED CURRY SOUP *makes about 6 or 8 cups*

#2
Combine

2 cans condensed green pea soup
2 cans tomato madrilene
¾ cup beef bouillon
½ cup dry white wine
1 tablespoon curry powder

Place over low heat and stir constantly until well blended. Remove from heat. Stir in

2 tablespoons lemon juice

Chill. If soup seems too thick, stir in about 1 cup of water. Just before serving stir in

½ cup unsweetened coconut, chopped or grated

Garnish, if desired, with

thinly sliced, unpeeled apple slices
grated coconut

REHOBOTH BEACH CHOWDER   *serves 8*

*#2

This is made with whatever fresh fish is available. It is very hearty. "Stolen" from Mrs. Mark O. Hatfield, who makes it with her home state's (Oregon) salmon.

Sauté until tender

> 1 small onion, chopped
> ¾ cup diced celery

in

> 4 tablespoons butter or margarine

Stir in

> ¼ cup flour

Slowly add

> 4½ cups milk

Continue stirring. Add

> 1¾ pounds fresh fish, skinned, boned, and cut up*
> 2 cups diced cooked potatoes
> 1 large plastic bag mixed vegetables (peas, carrots, corn, green beans, etc.)
> 1½ teaspoons fresh dill weed or ½ teaspoon dried
> 1½ teaspoons salt

Cook for 5 minutes. Freeze or refrigerate, if desired. To serve, cook until vegetables and fish are done. Adjust seasonings and serve steaming hot.

* If no fresh fish is available, canned salmon can be used.

SPINACH SOUP   *serves 8*

#2
Cook and drain

   1 (10-ounce) package frozen chopped spinach

Place in blender with some of

   4 cups light cream

Blend until smooth. Place

   4 chicken bouillon cubes

in remainder of cream and scald, stirring until cubes are dissolved.
Remove from heat. Stir in spinach mixture with

   ¼ cup dry vermouth
   1 teaspoon grated lemon rind
   ½ teaspoon mace

Chill. Serve topped with

   2 hard-cooked eggs, chopped

TOMATO LIME SOUP   *makes 6 cups*

#2
Combine and heat

>   2 cans condensed tomato soup
>   3 cups milk

Stirring constantly, heat until blended. Remove from heat. Add

>   1 cup heavy cream
>   1 tablespoon chopped fresh basil
> 1½ teaspoons soy sauce
>   2 tablespoons lime juice
> freshly ground black pepper

Mix well and chill thoroughly.
Serve ice cold sprinkled with

>   2 tablespoons chopped chives

Meat Dishes

BAKED CORNED BEEF *serves 8*

*#1
Look for a corned beef labeled for oven baking.

Bake at 325°

    1 (3½-pound) **corned beef**

After 2 hours remove from oven and sprinkle with mixture of

    pineapple juice
    brown sugar
    1 teaspoon dry mustard

Return to oven and bake another 45 minutes. Let stand 15 minutes before slicing. Or freeze, if desired, after the first 2 hours of baking. To serve, defrost and continue by coating with pineapple mixture and baking an additional 45 minutes.

Serve on

    soft rolls

BARBECUED BEEF ROAST
serves 10

#2
Combine in large bowl for marinade

    1 small onion, chopped
    1 cup vinegar
    ½ cup vegetable oil
    ⅓ cup light molasses
    ½ teaspoon dried basil
    ½ teaspoon celery salt
    ¼ teaspoon dried savory
    ¼ teaspoon garlic salt

In this, marinate for several hours (or up to 2 days)

    1 (4-pound) eye-of-the-round roast

There are several ways of cooking this meat. In the oven at home, you place it in a shallow roasting pan for 1½ to 2 hours at 325°, basting frequently. On a spit out of doors, it will take 1¼ to 1½ hours, basting frequently with the marinade. In a covered kettle cooker out of doors, it will take 1 hour. You may serve this hot or cold, sliced.

BARBECUED LAMB WITH PLUM SAUCE

serves 8

Drain, reserving syrup

    1 (1-pound 14-ounce) can purple plums

Pit plums and puree in blender with

    reserved syrup
    ¼ cup fresh lime juice
    1½ tablespoons soy sauce
    1 teaspoon Worcestershire sauce
    ¾ teaspoon dried basil
    1 clove garlic, crushed
    1½ tablespoons light corn syrup

Use this mixture (which may be made a day ahead) to baste during last hour of cooking

    1 (7-pound) leg of lamb

Lamb may be cooked on rotisserie spit or in covered kettle cooker until meat thermometer registers 175°. This will take 2½ to 3 hours.

CHILI CON SAUSAGE

serves 12

*#2

Sauté until meat browns

> 1½ pounds ground chuck
> 3 medium onions, chopped

in

> 3 tablespoons oil

Add

> 2 to 3 cloves garlic, minced
> 1 tablespoon ground cumin
> 2¼ teaspoons chili powder
> 1½ teaspoons paprika
> ¾ teaspoon freshly ground black pepper

When well blended, add

> 2 cups canned tomatoes

Meanwhile, in water to cover, simmer for 5 minutes

> 1½ pounds Polish, Spanish, or other spicy sausage

Remove casing from sausage, if necessary, and cut meat into small pieces. Add to tomato-beef mixture with

> 4½ (1-pound) cans kidney beans

and cook 15 to 20 minutes, until some of the liquid is absorbed. Adjust seasonings, if necessary. Refrigerate or freeze, if desired. To serve, reheat.

GRILLED SIRLOIN

Most commonly used for barbecuing is the sirloin steak. Select a dull red steak with streaks of fat running through the main portion. The best results are obtained when meat has been allowed to reach room temperature before grilling. Season with salt and pepper only after cooking. Score the fat of the border at 2-inch intervals without cutting the meat itself to prevent the meat from curling while it is cooking. When turning steak always use a pair of tongs as this will avoid piercing the meat and letting precious juices escape. Here is a chart to help you time your grilling over glowing coals. We prefer a covered cooker. Allow ¾ pound per person.

Time for covered cooker:

Thick-ness of Steak	Rare 1st side	Rare 2nd side	Medium 1st side	Medium 2nd side	Well Done 1st side	Well Done 2nd side
1-inch	4 min	5 min	5 min	6 min	6 min	7 min
2-inch	7 min	8 min	10 min	10 min	12 min	13 min
3-inch	17 min	18 min	24 min	24 min	27 min	28 min

Over open grill try these suggested times over white-hot coals:

	Broiling time each side	
	Rare	Medium
1-inch	5–7 min	7–10 min
1½-inch	7–10 min	10–13 min
2-inch	10–13 min	13–16 min

HAMBURGERS DIABLE

serves 8

#1
Combine for sauce

>   ½ cup mayonnaise
>   1 tablespoon prepared mustard
>   3 tablespoons chopped green pepper
>   2 tablespoons chopped pimiento
>   ½ teaspoon dried dill weed
>   ¼ teaspoon hot pepper sauce

Grill on one side only

>   16 unseasoned hamburger patties (4 pounds ground beef)

Turn and top patties with above sauce. Grill until done.

HONEY GLAZED SPARERIBS

serves 8

#3
Combine and simmer for 20 minutes

>   2 (8-ounce) cans tomato sauce
>   4 tablespoons wine vinegar
>   4 tablespoons minced onion
>   1 teaspoon salt
>   ½ teaspoon pepper
>   1 cup honey
>   2 cloves garlic, crushed

2 teaspoons Worcestershire sauce
2 teaspoons celery seed
1 cup dry sherry

Cut into pieces for serving

8 pounds spareribs

Parboil the ribs for 1 hour. Transfer to grill and cook over slow fire, basting frequently with sauce for 1 hour more.

LAMB CURRY

serves 8

#1
Combine

½ cup flour
2 to 3 tablespoons curry powder

Roll

4 pounds cubed lamb (chicken breasts or beef)

in this mixture and brown in skillet in

6 tablespoons butter

Blend in any remaining flour mixture. Add

1 can condensed onion soup
½ soup can of water
1 cup sliced celery
1 tart apple, peeled, cored, and coarsely chopped

    ¼ cup seedless raisins
    1 teaspoon lemon juice
    1 tablespoon lemon rind
    2 to 4 dashes hot pepper sauce

Cook over low heat for about 1 hour or until meat is tender. Stir often during cooking, adding more water if necessary. Refrigerate if desired. To serve, heat through either on the grill or on the stove. Just before serving, stir in

    ½ cup light cream

and heat again. Serve over hot rice with condiments, as many as you wish of those listed.

Condiments for "Eleven Boy Curry":
The term "eleven boy curry" means that 11 condiments are served with it. In India, when there were such things as dozens and dozens of servants, each condiment was served by a different servant.

    ½ cup dried currants soaked in ¼ cup port wine for
        at least 6 hours
    1 cup shredded coconut
    8 to 10 green onions, very thinly sliced
    ½ pound bacon, cooked crisp and crumbled
    2 ripe avocados, peeled, sliced, and sprinkled with lime
        juice (slice just before serving to prevent discoloration)
    1 medium jar chutney
    1 small can chopped toasted almonds
    1 cup diced green peppers
   16 pappadums (in place of bread) (Follow package
        directions. They may be prepared ahead.)
    bananas on the grill
    ½ cup golden seedless raisins soaked in ¼ cup brandy
        for at least 6 hours.

LONDON BROIL BÉARNAISE

serves 8

#1
Combine

    1 cup vegetable oil
    1 cup dry red wine
    4 tablespoons soy sauce
    2 tablespoons chopped green onion
    1 clove garlic, crushed
    1 teaspoon salt
    ¼ teaspoon pepper

Pour this over

    2 (2-pound) flank steaks

Marinate at least 4 hours or overnight. Broil steaks 5 minutes on each side, basting frequently with marinade. Slice thin on the diagonal. Serve with Béarnaise Sauce, if desired.

Béarnaise Sauce: *makes 1½ cups*
The Midas touch—worth the extra effort since it can be reheated.

Combine in small saucepan

    ¼ cup wine vinegar
    ¼ cup dry white wine
    1 tablespoon fresh tarragon or 1 teaspoon dried
    1 tablespoon minced green onions or shallots

Reduce, stirring, over high heat to about 2 tablespoons. Cool mixture and set aside. Meanwhile, in small saucepan, heat to boiling, but do not brown

½ cup butter

In blender place

   3 egg yolks
   2 tablespoons lemon juice
   ¼ teaspoon salt
   pinch of cayenne pepper

Cover container and flick motor off and on. Remove cover, turn on motor and add butter in steady stream until all added. Turn off motor immediately. Add to this mixture the 2 tablespoons vinegar-tarragon mixture. Blend well. Add

   1 more tablespoon minced fresh tarragon

Set aside. To warm, heat very slowly over hot water.

MEAT LOAF LOLLIPOPS   *serves 8*

*#2
Combine

   ½ cup tomato sauce with cheese
   2 eggs
   1 cup crushed pretzels
   4 tablespoons onion, chopped
   3 pounds ground chuck

Press mixture firmly into 24 medium muffin pans. Place on baking sheet. Bake at 350° for 20 minutes. Pour off fat.

Spoon additional

1½ cups tomato sauce

over meat. Bake 5 more minutes. Remove from muffin cups. Top each with

a pickle slice (24 in all)

Then push wooden skewer through pickle and firmly into meat to form lollipop. Chill before serving or serve at room temperature.

To make ahead, place in muffin pans and refrigerate or freeze. To serve, return to room temperature and bake as directed.

Note: 2 (8-ounce) cans tomato sauce equals 2 cups.

MICHAEL'S STEAK   *serves 6 to 8*

#3
Michael Burros "discovered" this one summer.

Combine

4 tablespoons butter
2 cloves garlic, crushed
juice of 1 lemon
1 cup tomato paste
1 cup Worcestershire sauce
freshly ground black pepper

Heat until bubbling. This may be refrigerated and heated again when ready for basting.

Sear a

6-to-8-pound sirloin steak, 3-inches thick

over hot coals. Each time steak is turned, baste with mixture. Baste lavishly. If there is any sauce left over, serve it heated, on the side.

MOUSSAKA À LA GRECQUE

serves 10 to 12

* #1
Authentic Greek recipe.

Peel and slice

> **3 slender eggplants**

Dip slices in

> **flour**

Fry quickly in

> **½ cup butter**
> **½ cup olive oil**

Season lightly with

> **salt and pepper**

Set aside. Heat in pan

> **4 tablespoons olive oil**

Cook until brown

  3 onions, finely chopped
  1 clove garlic, mashed

Add and cook for 10 minutes

  2 pounds ground chuck
  ½ pound ground lamb

Skim off fat. Combine

  3 tablespoons tomato paste
  1 (8-ounce) can tomato sauce
  ½ cup dry red wine
  ½ cup chopped fresh parsley
  1 tablespoon chopped fresh or dry mint
  ¼ teaspoon cinnamon
  1 tablespoon sugar
  salt and pepper

Add to meat and simmer over low heat until liquid is absorbed.
Make roux with

  8 tablespoons melted butter
  6 tablespoons flour

Blend in and bring to a boil

  1 quart milk

When thick and smooth, remove from heat. Cool slightly. Stir in

  4 eggs, beaten
  dash of nutmeg
  2 cups ricotta cheese

Grease an 11-by-16-inch pan and sprinkle bottom with

bread crumbs (use 1 cup total in recipe)

Arrange in layers eggplant and meat sauce and over each layer sprinkle

grated Parmesan cheese (use 1 cup total)
bread crumbs

Pour cheese sauce over top and bake at 375° for 1 hour. Remove from oven and cool ½ hour before serving. Cut into squares. Or after thorough cooling may be frozen. Thaw about 4 hours and reheat in 325° oven until heated through.

Note: To carry to picnic, wrap in heavy duty foil and reheat on top of grill.

NORWEGIAN MEAT PIE   *serves 6*

#1
This is a recipe from Cape Cod. It is delightful warm and almost as good cold.

Blend together

2½ **pounds ground round**
 2 **slices pumpernickel or rye bread, diced very small**
 1 **teaspoon caraway seed**
 1 **teaspoon salt**

Pat this mixture very firmly into a 10-inch pie plate or shallow casserole to form a pie crust. Reserve 3 to 4 tablespoons of mixture. Bake crust at 300° for about 30 minutes, until lightly browned. Remove from oven and pour off any excess fat. If crust has developed any holes, patch with reserved meat mixture. Sprinkle over bottom of crust

3 ounces Gruyere cheese, diced

Sprinkle over cheese

1 celery stalk, sliced thinly
1 green onion, sliced thinly

At this point, the dish may be refrigerated. To serve, return to room temperature. Beat together lightly with fork

4 eggs
1 pint light cream or half-and-half

Bake at 350° for 45 minutes, until filling is set. Time will depend on size of pan. If crust seems to be browning too much, cover it with aluminum foil. Remove from oven and allow to set at least 15 minutes before slicing to serve.

PICADINHO

serves 12

*#2
Heat in large skillet

2 tablespoons olive or salad oil

Add

2 medium onions, chopped
3 pounds ground chuck

Sauté until meat is well browned. Add

4 cans tomato slices
1½ teaspoons dried oregano
1½ teaspoons salt
½ teaspoon freshly ground black pepper
½ cup sliced pimiento-stuffed olives

Simmer 30 minutes. Add

8 ounces shredded Cheddar cheese

Cover and cook until cheese melts. Do not stir. Just before serving add

2 medium-sized boiled potatoes, peeled and diced
4 hard-cooked eggs, sliced

Serve over cooked rice.
To prepare ahead, simmer 30 minutes; then refrigerate or freeze. To serve, return to room temperature, heat through, and continue with directions.

PIC-L-NIC BEEF ROLL   *serves 6 to 8*

#1
Spread

2 flank steaks (weighing together about 3 pounds)

with

prepared hot mustard

Sprinkle with

seasoned salt
pepper

Starting at narrow end, alternate rows of

6 to 8 dill pickles, quartered lengthwise
4 to 5 carrots, quartered lengthwise
6 to 8 green onions, quartered lengthwise

on top of steaks. Roll up jelly-roll fashion and tie securely with strings at 1-inch intervals. Brown steaks on all sides in heavy skillet or Dutch oven in

hot shortening

Pour off drippings. Add

1 cup water
2 beef bouillon cubes
¼ cup vinegar
2 cups dry red wine
1 teaspoon whole black peppercorns
2 bay leaves
4 sprigs parsley
2 stalks celery cut in 2-inch pieces

Cover and cook about 2½ hours or until meat is tender. Allow meat to cool in liquid; then cover and chill overnight. To serve, remove meat from liquid and remove strings. Cut diagonally into slices about 1-inch thick. Spread

8 seeded split rolls

with

butter
mustard or mayonnaise

To serve, fill rolls with the sliced meat.

POOR BOY SANDWICHES OR
ROMAN GRINDERS   *2 or 3 servings per loaf*

Slice horizontally and remove insides from

2 (18-inch) loaves Italian or French bread

Spread inside top and bottom halves with

mayonnaise
sweet pickle relish

Cover the bottom layers of the loaves with

2 pounds sliced salami
2 layers sliced tomatoes
½ pound sliced Mortadella or well-seasoned bologna
2 (8-ounce) packages sliced Provolone cheese
4 (2-ounce) cans marinated mushrooms, drained

Place top halves on loaves and wrap grinders tightly. These may be put together a couple of hours before serving, or the makings may be carried to the picnic site, and the grinders put together there.

ROAST BEEF CALIFORNIAN   *serves 6 to 8*

#1
In a deep bowl place

   1 (3-pound) rolled beef rump roast

Combine

   1 cup orange juice
   1 cup tomato juice
   ¼ cup salad oil
   2 teaspoons salt
   1 clove garlic, crushed
   ½ teaspoon allspice
   ½ teaspoon chili powder

Pour this mixture over roast. Refrigerate, covered, overnight.
Turn roast occasionally; remove from marinade and roast at 300°
to 325°, 25 minutes to the pound, basting occasionally with
remaining marinade. Cool and slice thinly. Serve at room
temperature.

SOUTH AFRICAN SHISH KEBOB   *serves 6 to 8*

#1
Cut into 1½-inch cubes

   3 pounds boneless lamb

Chop and sauté

> 2 medium onions

in

> 2 tablespoons salad oil

Combine with

> 1 tablespoon curry powder
> 2 tablespoons vinegar
> 1 bay leaf
> 2 teaspoons chili powder
> 1 teaspoon salt
> 1 clove garlic, crushed
> 2 (12-ounce) cans apricot nectar

Simmer sauce for 10 minutes and pour over meat to marinate 3 to 4 hours or overnight. Thread meat on skewers and broil over hot coals until done to your liking (about 40 minutes). Just before removing from grill, baste meat with remaining marinade.

SOUTHWESTERN LAMB
serves 8

Have your butcher bone

> 6-to-7-pound leg of lamb

Open meat out flat (*butterfly it*) and marinate it for 8 to 24 hours in a mixture of

   1 cup dry red wine
   ½ cup orange juice
   ¼ cup chili sauce
   ¼ cup water
   1 onion, minced
   2 tablespoons olive oil
   1 tablespoon chili powder
   1 tablespoon brown sugar
   1 teaspoon crushed cumin seed
   ¾ teaspoon dried oregano
   ½ teaspoon salt
   ½ teaspoon pepper

Drain meat, reserving marinade for basting. Broil on grill, 4 to 6 inches from heat, basting frequently. It will take about 45 minutes for meat to be done, still slightly pink as lamb should be served.

Poultry
Dishes

CALYPSO CHICKEN BARBECUE

serves 8

Place in shallow baking pan

2 broilers, cut into serving pieces

Dot chicken with

½ cup butter

Sprinkle with

> salt
> paprika

Bake at 350° for 1 hour. Refrigerate, if desired. When ready to serve, cover chicken with Barbecue Sauce and broil either indoors or preferably outdoors on grill until crusty and brown.

* #2
Barbecue Sauce:

In a heavy saucepan heat

> ½ cup olive oil

In it sauté until wilted

> 1 onion, finely chopped
> 1 clove garlic, crushed

Add

> 2 cups chili sauce
> 1 cup catsup
> ½ teaspoon dried oregano
> ½ teaspoon celery seed
> 1 tablespoon Dijon mustard
> 1 tablespoon wine vinegar
> ½ teaspoon black pepper
> salt to taste
> a few drops of hot pepper sauce
> ¼ teaspoon ground cumin

Bring to a boil, reduce heat, simmer 10 minutes. Stir in

> ⅓ cup dark rum

CHICKEN GAUGUIN
serves 8 to 10

#1
Toss to combine

    6 **cups cooked chicken, cut in bite-sized pieces**
    3 **cups orange sections**
    ⅔ **cup flaked coconut**

Blend together

    3 **ounces cream cheese**
    ¾ **cup heavy cream**
    ¼ **cup orange juice**
    1½ **teaspoons curry powder**
    1 **teaspoon salt**
    2 **tablespoons chutney**

Add dressing to chicken and toss. Serve in

    lettuce cups

CHICKEN IN TUNA SAUCE
serves 8

#1
Combine in heavy saucepan

    4 **large chicken breasts, halved and skinned**
    1¼ **cups dry white wine**
    1 **onion, finely chopped**
    1 **clove garlic, finely chopped**
    1 **(7-ounce) can tuna**

6 anchovy fillets, chopped
½ teaspoon salt
¼ teaspoon freshly ground black pepper
1 teaspoon grated lemon rind

Cover and bring to boil; simmer gently 25 minutes or until chicken is tender. Slice the chicken into large oval pieces, discarding bones. Transfer to a bowl. Puree the sauce in which the chicken was cooked in an electric blender or food mill. Add

¼ cup olive oil
3 tablespoons lemon juice
6 tablespoons mayonnaise

Pour over the chicken and cover. Let stand overnight. Carry separately to picnic with

4 cups cold, cooked rice
½ jar capers
3 tablespoons chopped parsley
2 pints cherry tomatoes
1 lemon, sliced

At picnic, arrange rice on platter. Place chicken pieces on top of rice. Spoon sauce over all and sprinkle with parsley and capers. Surround with cherry tomatoes and lemon slices.

CHICKEN PINEAPPLE SALAD   *serves 8*

#1
Cook in salted water for 1 hour or until tender

1 (5-pound) stewing chicken
few sprigs of parsley

slices of lemon
1 small onion, sliced
2 stalks celery
½ teaspoon dried dill weed

Cool in broth, then remove skin and bones from chicken. Cut into bite-sized pieces. Toss chicken with

3 cups cubed, fresh pineapple
1 cup cooked, diced celery
1 cup chopped water chestnuts
½ cup mayonnaise
¼ cup sour cream
½ teaspoon salt
¼ teaspoon pepper
¼ teaspoon sugar
½ clove garlic, crushed
1 teaspoon celery seed

Serve in lettuce cups. Garnish with

¼ cup coarsely chopped, toasted almonds

CURRIED CHICKEN AND BROCCOLI
serves 8

*#2
This recipe is a favorite of such politically diverse people as Ginny Tydings, wife of the former Democratic senator from Maryland, and Julie Nixon Eisenhower.

Cook; then skin, bone, and slice

4 whole chicken breasts

Cook and drain

2 packages frozen broccoli

Place broccoli in casserole, sprinkle with salt, and top with slices of chicken meat. Combine

1 can condensed cream of chicken soup
⅔ cup mayonnaise
⅓ cup evaporated milk
½ cup grated American cheese
1 teaspoon lemon juice
½ teaspoon curry powder

Pour over chicken and sprinkle with

1 cup buttered bread crumbs

Refrigerate or freeze, if desired. To serve, return to room temperature and bake at 350° for 25 to 30 minutes, until bubbly and hot.

ERNIE'S CHICKEN PROVENÇAL   *serves 12*

* #2
Heat in heavy skillet

¾ cup olive oil

Pat dry on paper towels

12 pounds cut up chicken parts

Brown in hot oil. Stir in

> 3 tablespoons chopped garlic
> 3¼ cups peeled, seeded, and chopped tomatoes
> 3 tablespoons flour

Mix well and add

> 1½ cups dry white wine
> 3 cups chicken broth or bouillon

Add

> 3 small bay leaves
> ¾ teaspoon dried thyme
> ¾ teaspoon dried rosemary
> salt and pepper to taste

Refrigerate or freeze if desired. To serve, return to room temperature, cover, and simmer 30 to 40 minutes or until chicken tests done.
Add

> 1½ cups pitted black olives

Cook 5 minutes more and serve.

FARMER IN THE DELL
serves 12

#2
Roll

> 6 cups diced cooked chicken

in mixture of

flour
salt and pepper

Brown in

½ pound butter

Meanwhile, cook for 7 to 8 minutes

6 **medium tomatoes, cut up**
3 **green peppers, chopped**
3 **onions, chopped**
1 **small bunch parsley, chopped**
1 **stalk celery, chopped**

until celery is tender but crisp. Combine the browned chicken with the vegetables and

¼ **pound currants or raisins**
1½ **teaspoons curry powder**

To serve, heat through and sprinkle with

¼ **pound toasted, slivered almonds**

Serve with

canned Chinese fried noodles on plain rice

Dish may be prepared ahead and reheated, topped with almonds.

GRILLED LIME CHICKEN   *serves 6*

#1
The chicken preparation can be done a day ahead. The grilling is done just before serving.

Rub both sides

2 (3-pound) broilers, cut in serving pieces

with

lime juice
paprika
seasoned salt

Marinate in refrigerator for several hours or overnight. Just before cooking, sprinkle with more

paprika
seasoned salt

Combine

½ cup melted butter
4 tablespoons lime juice

Brush chicken pieces with lime butter and cook chicken over hot coals on grill, brushing with lime butter as it cooks. Turn occasionally.

NANCY'S CHICKEN AND RICE SALAD

serves 6 to 8

#1
Cook one day ahead

2 cups rice

Rinse and refrigerate. Add

3 cups cooked, diced chicken or turkey
1 cup slivered almonds
½ cup minced onion

Combine

1½ cups mayonnaise
3 tablespoons curry powder
¼ cup soy sauce
2 tablespoons vinegar

Mix the rice-chicken mixture with the dressing and chill thoroughly. Decorate with pimientos to serve.

PICNIC FRIED CHICKEN   *serves 6*

*#2
Cut into serving pieces

2 (2½–3-pound) broiler-fryers

Moisten with

½ cup water

Shake off excess. Combine

3 cups Italian seasoned bread crumbs
½ cup finely chopped pecans
1 cup grated Parmesan cheese

Place some of mixture in plastic bag and toss a few pieces of chicken in the mixture at a time; repeat. Arrange coated chicken . skin-side-up in a single layer on ungreased shallow baking pan. Bake at 400° for 40 to 50 minutes or until chicken is tender and coating crisp. Serve hot or cold.

Freeze, if desired, before baking. Return to room temperature before cooking.

SESAME CHICKEN   *serves 8*

*#1
Combine

> 1⅓ cups fine, salted soda cracker crumbs
> ½   cup sesame seeds, toasted

Dip

> 2 (3-pound) broilers, cut up

in

> ⅔ cup evaporated milk

Then roll in crumb mixture. Pour into a 9-by-13-inch baking dish

> 1 cup melted butter

Dip skin side of chicken pieces in butter, turn over and arrange skin-side-up in baking dish. Bake at 375° for 1 hour. Cool. Chill or freeze. To serve, return to room temperature.

WENTE CHICKEN

serves 6 to 8

#2
Created by the owner of Wente Vineyards on the spot, when he was challenged to prove he could cook.

Season

   2 (3-pound) broilers, cut up

with

   salt and pepper

Dredge lightly in

   flour

In heavy pan, heat

   4 tablespoons butter or margarine

Brown chicken quickly on all sides. Transfer to casserole. Then add

   ½ onion, sliced
   2 cloves garlic

Tie together with string

   4 sprigs parsley
   4 stalks celery

Add to chicken. Sprinkle with

¼ teaspoon dried thyme
¼ teaspoon dried marjoram
¼ teaspoon dried rosemary

Pour into frying pan

2 cups dry white wine

Scrape sides and bottom of pan and pour all over chicken. Cut into quarters

2 tomatoes

Add to casserole and cover. Bake at 350° for 30 minutes. Add

½ pound fresh mushrooms

Cook 10 minutes longer, uncovered. Remove celery, parsley, and garlic. Serve hot. This can be prepared ahead and refrigerated. To serve, bring to room temperature and reheat until hot all the way through.
Note: This can also be done on the top of the grill.

Seafood Dishes

COLD SALMON—SAUCE VERTE

serves 6 to 8

#1
Simmer together for ½ hour

- 1 onion
- 2 stalks celery
- 1 cup water
- ¼ teaspoon salt
- 3 pounds fresh salmon, cut into 8 steaks or left in one piece

Cool. Serve cold with Sauce Verte on the side.

Sauce Verte:

Fold

> 1 tablespoon minced fresh chives
> 1 tablespoon dried tarragon leaves or 3 tablespoons fresh
> 2 tablespoons fresh minced parsley
> 1 teaspoon dried chervil, finely chopped
> 1 teaspoon dried dill weed, minced or 3 teaspoons fresh

into

> 2 cups mayonnaise

Chill.

DANISH LOAF
serves 8

#1
Worth the advance preparation.

Remove all crusts and slice horizontally into 5 slices

> 1 white bread sandwich loaf, unsliced

Spread slices with

> softened butter

Flake

   ½ pound crabmeat

Mix it with

   1 tablespoon mayonnaise
   1 tablespoon sour cream

Spread filling evenly on 1 slice.
Combine for spread on second slice

   2 hard-cooked eggs, chopped
   1 tablespoon mayonnaise
   1 tablespoon sour cream
   ¼ teaspoon Dijon mustard
   dash of seasoned salt

Combine and spread on third slice

   3 ounces cream cheese
   1 tablespoon sour cream
   ½ teaspoon dried tarragon, crumbled

Brush fourth slice with

   2 teaspoons mayonnaise
   2 teaspoons sour cream

Top this slice with contents of

   1 (3½-ounce) can small sardines, drained

Stack the sandwich layers, topping with the final piece of bread.
Whip together

   8 ounces softened cream cheese
   ¼ cup sour cream

Use to frost sides and top of loaf. Garnish with

> **radish roses**
> **parsley**

Chill until served.

LOBSTER LUNCHEON SALAD *serves 6 to 8*

#1
Cook and drain

> **2 cups elbow macaroni**

Toss macaroni with

> **1 pound cooked lobster meat**
> **¼ cup garlic French dressing**
> **1 cup raw cauliflowerets**
> **½ cup sliced green onions**
> **½ cup sliced pimiento-stuffed olives**
> **½ cup sliced ripe olives**
> **½ cup marinated artichoke hearts, drained**
> **½ cup mayonnaise**

Chill. Serve in bowl lined with

> **watercress**

Decorate with

> **capers**

MARYLAND CRABCAKES   *serves 8*

#1
Pick over and then mix

    3 pounds lump crabmeat

with

    1½ cups cracker crumbs

Combine

    6 tablespoons mayonnaise
    3 tablespoons prepared mustard
    3 beaten eggs
    3 tablespoons chopped parsley
    1 tablespoon Worcestershire sauce

Blend this mixture carefully with crabmeat. Do not break up lumps of crabmeat. Form into 18 patties. Refrigerate, if desired. When ready to serve, pan fry in

    butter

until golden brown.

ORIENTAL SALMON STEAKS   *serves 8*

#1
Combine in a quart container with tight-fitting lid

    2 packages garlic French dressing mix
   ½ cup water
   ½ cup soy sauce
   ⅔ cup lemon juice
    2 teaspoons ground ginger

Shake well. Pour over

    8 salmon steaks, 1-inch thick

Marinate for several hours or overnight. Broil or grill as desired 4 to 5 minutes on each side.

PAIN BAGNAT
(French Picnic Sandwich) *makes 2 or 3*

Slice horizontally and remove insides from

    1 (18-inch) loaf Italian or French bread

On lower half arrange

    8 slices tomatoes
   ¾ cup thinly sliced green onions
  1½ (7-ounce) cans tuna fish, flaked
   ½ (6-ounce) can pitted black olives, sliced

Spread over

    3 tablespoons mayonnaise

Sprinkle with

    1½ teaspoons wine vinegar
    ½ teaspoon freshly ground black pepper
    ½ jar capers, drained
    1½ cans flat anchovies, drained

Cover with top half and wrap tightly. These may be made 2 hours ahead or all the makings can be carried to picnic site, and the sandwiches made there.

RED SNAPPER WITH
TOMATO SAUCE

serves 6

#1

Called Huachinango Veracruzano in Mexico, it is served with boiled potatoes and chiles largos, if they can be found.

Pour

    juice of 1 lime

over

    2 pounds red snapper fillets, ½-inch thick

Let stand while making sauce. Sauté until golden

    1 medium onion , diced
    2 cloves garlic, sliced

in

    1 tablespoon oil

Add

3 small tomatoes, peeled, seeded, and diced
1 canned pimiento, chopped
2 canned chiles serranos, rinsed in cold water and sliced
1 tablespoon capers
12 pitted green olives
¼ cup dry sherry
4 tablespoons cider vinegar
½ teaspoon chili powder (optional)
½ teaspoon oregano
⅛ teaspoon cinnamon
1 teaspoon salt
¼ teaspoon pepper

Cook until thickened, about 10 minutes. Place fillets in greased baking dish; pour sauce over. Cover. Refrigerate if desired. To serve, bake at 350° for about 30 minutes, if refrigerated; 20 minutes, if not. Serve with chiles largos and boiled potatoes.

SAUMON EN CROUTE   *serves 6*

#1
The fancy title just means salmon in a crust.

In skillet melt

2 tablespoons butter

Sauté until tender

   1 cup finely chopped onions
   ½ cup green pepper, chopped
   1 (4-ounce) can mushroom stems and pieces, drained

Combine

   1 (1-pound) can salmon and its liquid
   5 hard-cooked eggs, finely chopped
   ¼ teaspoon freshly ground black pepper
   ½ teaspoon salt
   1 teaspoon dried dill weed or tarragon (or 1 tablespoon
     fresh)
   2 tablespoons chopped parsley

Stir in vegetable mixture and combine thoroughly, but lightly.
On lightly floured board, line up in 2 rows of 3 each (sides
touching)

   1 package puff pastry patty shells (defrosted overnight
     in the refrigerator)

Roll into a 12-inch square. Pile filling on one half of square,
leaving 1-inch margin on three sides. Fold uncovered portion of
dough over filling and pinch edges of dough together firmly.
Roll onto baking sheet so seam is on bottom and reshape into
loaf with hands. Brush with mixture of

   1 egg beaten with 1 tablespoon water

Prick top at regular intervals with a fork and refrigerate 30
minutes before baking. Bake at 425° for 30 to 40 minutes or until
crust is golden brown. Refrigerate. Serve chilled with Lemon
Mayonnaise—made by combining mayonnaise with lemon juice
and grated rind to taste.

Vegetables

BANANAS ON THE GRILL

Condiment for Curry.

For 1 serving, wash and dry

1 green banana, unpeeled

Place on grill 4 inches from medium coals. Cook 20 minutes, turning once or until peel is black and banana soft. Split and sprinkle with

confectioners' sugar

Serve in peel.

BEA'S RATATOUILLE

serves 12

#3

Our Friday morning tennis group gets together for mixed doubles and supper occasionally. This was Bea Prosterman's contribution.

Scrub and trim but do not peel

4 large ripe eggplants

Cut into 1-inch cubes.
Scrub and trim

6 medium zucchini

Cut into ¼-inch thick slices.
Slice

6 medium onions

Wash and seed

6 green peppers

Cut into 1-inch pieces. Peel and put through press or mince fine

5 cloves garlic

Discard tough stems of

15 sprigs fresh dill*
12 sprigs fresh parsley

Place these ingredients in a pot along with

2 teaspoons dried oregano
1 (2-pound 3-ounce) can peeled Italian tomatoes
3 tablespoons salt
½ teaspoon freshly ground black pepper
¼ cup salad oil

With large wooden spoon, mix contents of pot until coated with oil and seasonings are distributed. Cover and bake at 350°. Stir fairly frequently in the beginning until vegetables soften and juices begin to flow. After that, stir occasionally and bake 3 hours. Leave cover off during last ½ hour of cooking and stir.

Serve hot or cold. If serving hot, reheat when ready to serve.

BROILED SEASONED TOMATOES   *makes 8*

#1
Cut in half

4 large ripe tomatoes

Sprinkle cut sides with

seasoned salt

Broil several inches from heat until tops begin to brown and tomatoes are heated through.

* If fresh dill is not available, substitute 2½ teaspoons dried dill weed.

ELKRIDGE TOMATOES

serves 8

#1
Combine

> ⅓ **cup cornmeal**
> ⅓ **cup flour**
> 1 **teaspoon salt**
> ½ **teaspoon pepper**

Heat in skillet

> ¼ **cup bacon fat**

Slice into 1-inch thick slices

> 6 **firm medium tomatoes**

Dip these slices in cornmeal mixture and sauté quickly on both sides until brown in bacon fat. Use more fat, if necessary. Sprinkle slices on both sides with

> 2 **tablespoons brown sugar**

Drain tomatoes and layer in shallow greased casserole with slices overlapping. Refrigerate, if desired. To serve, return to room temperature and bake at 350° for about 20 minutes, or until heated through.

GREEN ONION PIE   *serves 8*

* #1

Crust:

Combine with pastry blender or two forks until crumbly

>   1 cup sifted flour
> ½ teaspoon salt
> ½ teaspoon sugar
> ½ cup butter

Blend in

>   2 tablespoons cold milk

Form into ball and refrigerate for 1 hour until dough can be rolled out. Roll to fill a 9-inch plate. Flute edges and prick all over.

Filling:

Sauté for 5 minutes

>   3 cups thinly sliced green onions with tops

in

> ¼ cup butter

Season with

>   1 teaspoon salt
> ⅛ teaspoon pepper
> dash of cayenne pepper
> ½ teaspoon caraway seeds

Blend in

> 1 **cup milk**
> 1 **cup sour cream**
> 2 **eggs**

Pour into pie shell. Refrigerate or freeze. When ready to serve, return to room temperature and bake at 400° for 15 minutes. Reduce heat to 350° and bake 30 to 40 minutes more until set.

LEMON ZUCCHINI

serves 8

#1
Colorful as well as tasty.

In large skillet, sauté until just tender

> 6 **cups (about 3 pounds) zucchini cut in ½-inch slices**
> 3 **cups whole cherry tomatoes**

in

> 3 **tablespoons butter**

Add and mix with vegetables

> 1½ **teaspoons lemon-pepper**
> ¾ **teaspoon salt**

Meanwhile brown

> 1½ **cups bread crumbs**

in

3 tablespoons butter

Add

1½ tablespoons grated lemon rind

Place zucchini and tomatoes in shallow 3-quart baking dish. Top with crumb mixture. Refrigerate if desired. To serve, heat thoroughly at 400° for 10 to 15 minutes.

ROASTED CORN ON THE COB   *serves 8*

Soak in water for 10 minutes

8 ears freshly picked corn with husks left on

Roast ears over hot coals for 15 to 20 minutes, turning once. Strip away husks. Butter well. Sprinkle with

salt

ZUCCHINI WITH SOUR CREAM   *serves 8*

#1
Scrub but do not peel

    4 pounds young zucchini

Cut them crosswise into 1-inch slices. Drop them into

    2 inches boiling water
    1 teaspoon salt
    ½ teaspoon lemon-pepper
    1 tablespoon minced onion

Cook them covered until they are tender. Drain well. Pour over
zucchini and mix gently

    2 tablespoons butter
    1 cup sour cream

May be reheated at serving time.

Potato, Noodle, and Rice Dishes

ALMOND CRUNCH RICE

serves 8

Sauté until slightly browned

1 cup diced almonds

in

4 tablespoons melted butter

Toss together

6 cups cooked rice
1 cup shredded Gruyère cheese

with the almonds and butter. Season to taste. Serve hot.

BAKED POTATOES FLORENTINE   *serves 8*

#1
Bake at 450° for 55 to 60 minutes

8 well-scrubbed baking potatoes

Cook as directed on package

2 (9-ounce) packages frozen creamed spinach

Cut small lengthwise slice from top of each potato and scoop out pulp. Combine

pulp
3 egg yolks
4 tablespoons butter
2 teaspoons salt
½ teaspoon pepper
½ teaspoon onion powder
½ teaspoon nutmeg

Beat until smooth. Stir in drained spinach. Heap back into shells. Cut into 2 strips each

4 slices processed Cheddar cheese

Place one strip on each potato. Place on cookie sheet and return to 450° oven for 8 to 10 minutes until cheese melts and potato is hot. When carrying to a picnic, wrap potatoes in foil and reheat on top of grill.

CHINESE RICE CASSEROLE

serves 6

*#1
Melt in skillet

    6 tablespoons butter or margarine

Add

    1 medium onion, finely chopped
    1 clove garlic, mashed
    1 medium green pepper, finely chopped

Cook over moderate heat until tender. Stir in

    1 cup raw rice

Cook over moderate heat until lightly browned, stirring occasionally. Add

    1 (4-ounce) can mushroom stems and pieces
    2 tablespoons soy sauce
    1 teaspoon dried oregano

Reduce heat and simmer 20 minutes, stirring occasionally. Pour rice mixture into 1½-quart casserole and add

1 (12½-ounce) can chicken consommé or broth
¾ cup water

Cover and bake at 350° for 1¼ hours. Or freeze or refrigerate
before baking. To serve, return to room temperature and bake at
350°, but check after 1 hour. Since much of the liquid has been
absorbed by the rice, it has done some cooking without being
in the oven.

CONFETTI RICE   *serves 10*

#1
Cook until tender

    1 cup sliced fresh mushrooms
    ½ cup chopped onion

in

    ⅓ cup butter

Add to mushrooms and onion

    4 cups hot cooked rice (1⅓ cups raw rice)
    1 (10-ounce) package frozen peas, undercooked and
      drained
    1 teaspoon salt
    ¼ teaspoon pepper
    ¼ teaspoon crushed dried rosemary

Heat, stirring. Sprinkle with

    ¼ cup slivered almonds, toasted

Refrigerate. When ready to serve, reheat in top of double boiler. Carry to picnic in thermal casserole or keep warm for backyard barbecue on an electric hot tray.

CURRIED RICE

serves 8

#1
Melt

½ cup butter

Add

1 teaspoon curry powder

Sauté in butter

½ pound mushrooms, sliced
2 tablespoons chopped green pepper
2 tablespoons chopped onion

Add

½ cup pecans, coarsely chopped

Cook for 1 minute, then add

3 cups chicken broth
1½ cups long-grain rice

Place in 2-quart casserole. Refrigerate. When ready to serve, bake at 325° until liquid is absorbed, about 1 hour.

HOT POTATO SALAD   *serves 8*

#1
Melt in a large frying pan

    2 tablespoons butter

Cook in butter until tender

    1 cup thinly sliced celery
    ¼ cup sliced green onion

Combine, then add to celery mixture

    2 tablespoons flour
    2 tablespoons sugar
    2 teaspoons salt
    1 teaspoon paprika
    1 teaspoon dry mustard
    ¼ teaspoon pepper

Stir in gradually, until thickened

    1 cup milk

Then stir in

    ¼ cup vinegar

Add and stir to coat with dressing

    4 cups sliced, boiled potatoes
    ½ cup diced green pepper

Refrigerate if desired. To serve, heat slowly and stir in

> ½ cup sour cream

Sprinkle with

> 4 slices bacon, fried crisp and crumbled

MACARONI PICNIC BOWL   *serves 6*

#2
Cook according to package directions

> 1 (8-ounce) package elbow macaroni

Drain, rinse in cold water, and drain again.
Cook according to package directions

> 1 (10-ounce) package frozen peas and carrots

Drain and combine with

> macaroni
> 4 ounces diced Cheddar cheese (1 cup)
> ⅓ cup sliced celery

Cover and chill. Combine

> ⅓ cup vinegar
> ⅓ cup salad oil
> ⅓ cup water
> 2 teaspoons sugar

    1½ **teaspoons salt**
    ½ **teaspoon dried marjoram**
    ½ **teaspoon dried chervil**

Beat or shake thoroughly and pour over macaroni mixture.
Toss well and chill at least a few hours. Decorate with
    cherry tomatoes

NOODLES ITALIENNE   *serves 8*

#1
Cook according to package direction, then drain

    1 **(12-ounce) package spinach noodles**

Drain reserving juice from

    1 **pound crabmeat**

Melt

    6 **tablespoons butter**

Stir in

    6 **tablespoons flour**

Gradually stir in

    1 **cup light cream**

To reserved juice add

enough beer to make 2 cups

Gradually stir this into cream. Cook over low heat, stirring, until thick and bubbly. Stir in

**crabmeat
½ cup sliced, pitted black olives
¼ cup chopped pimiento**

Pour sauce over noodles. Sprinkle with

1 cup grated Provolone cheese

When ready to serve, bake at 350° for 40 minutes.

POTATOES IN ARMOR   *serves 8*

Cut into ½-inch slices, crosswise, but not quite through,

8 medium baking potatoes, peeled

Blend together

**1 cup softened butter
4 teaspoons seasoned salt
4 teaspoons seasoned pepper**

Spread butter mixture between slices. Wrap each potato in heavy duty aluminum foil, closing securely. Arrange potatoes on grill over medium heat. Cook for 30 minutes. Turn and cook for 30 minutes more, or until potatoes are easily pierced with a fork.

SUNSHINE PASTA

serves 8

#2
Cook according to package directions and drain

    1 (1-pound) package elbow macaroni

Melt

    4 tablespoons butter

Add and blend in

    4 tablespoons flour

Off heat, blend in

    2 cups milk

Return to low heat and cook, stirring until thickened. Add and mix well

    ½ cup Italian or French dressing, homemade or bottled
    10 tablespoons orange juice concentrate, undiluted

Combine the macaroni with

    16 slices bacon, cooked and crumbled
    ⅔ cup sliced, pitted black olives
    ½ cup chopped toasted almonds
    salt and pepper to taste
    2 medium oranges, sliced

Then add the Italian dressing mixture. Place in casserole and refrigerate, if desired. To serve, return to room temperature and bake at 350° for 40 to 50 minutes or until hot through. Garnish with

cooked bacon slices (optional)

TENE'S NOODLE PUDDING   *serves 8 to 10*

* #2
Boil as directed, rinse, and drain

1 (8-ounce) package fine noodles

Cream together

**¾ cup butter
3 (3-ounce) packages cream cheese
1 pint sour cream
½ teaspoon salt
6 tablespoons sugar
1½ teaspoons lemon juice**

Beat in

4 eggs

Add noodles to cream mixture. Pour into 9-by-13-inch pan. Refrigerate or freeze. When ready to serve, return to room temperature and bake at 350° for 1 hour. Remove from oven, cut into serving pieces.

Salads
and Cold
Vegetables

ARMENIAN SALAD   *serves 8*

#1
Combine and bring to a boil

>   1 cup bulghur wheat
>   2 cups cold water
>   1 teaspoon salt

Reduce heat, cover tightly, and simmer 15 minutes. Pour over
bulghur

　　½　cup French dressing

Chill for at least 1 hour or overnight. Add to bulghur

　　　2　tablespoons diced green pepper
　　　¼　cup chopped chives or green onions
　　　½　cup diced celery
　　　8　pimiento-stuffed green olives, sliced
　　1½　pounds cooked, cleaned shrimp, halved
　　12　cherry tomatoes, halved
　　　¼　cup mayonnaise

Serve on

　　crisp salad greens

AVOCADO AND MELON SALAD　　　*serves 6 to 8*

#1
Dressing:

Slice

　　½　pint strawberries

whirl them in blender until smooth with

　　1½　cups sour cream
　　　¼　teaspoon salt
　　　¼　teaspoon grated lemon rind

Chill.

Salad:

Arrange on lettuce-lined platter

    3 avocados, sliced and dipped in lemon juice
    6 cups mixed fresh melon balls
    ½ pint whole strawberries
    1 pound creamed cottage cheese

Serve with dressing. Garnish with

    fresh mint leaves

BROCCOLI FLOWERS

#1
Beautiful as well as delicious.

Cut into flowerets

    1 bunch fresh broccoli

Drop broccoli into boiling water for 1 minute to blanch. Remove from water and chill well. To serve, place broccoli on plate surrounding a bowl of Lemon-Mayonnaise.

Lemon-Mayonnaise:

Combine and chill

½ cup mayonnaise
juice of one lemon
grated rind of one lemon

Note: Both broccoli and lemon-mayonnaise should be kept in refrigerator until serving time.

BROCCOLI VINAIGRETTE   *serves 8*

#1
Cook in boiling salted water until tender

2 bunches fresh broccoli

Drain, chill, and serve with Vinaigrette Sauce.

#3
Vinaigrette Sauce:

Combine and chill

    ½ **cup olive oil**
    4 **tablespoons tarragon vinegar**
    1 **tablespoon chopped sweet pickle**
    1 **hard-cooked egg, riced**
    1 **teaspoon minced chives**
    2 **tablespoons chopped parsley**
    1 **pimiento, chopped**
  salt and pepper to taste

CHICK-PEA SALAD

serves 6

#2
Combine

    2 (1-pound 4-ounce) cans chick-peas, drained
    1 medium onion, chopped
    ½ cup sliced sweet gherkins
    ½ cup sweet pickle liquid
    ½ teaspoon salt
    dash of pepper
    3 tablespoons wine vinegar
    2 pimientos, cut up

Mix lightly and chill at least overnight. Garnish with additional pimiento, if desired.

COLE SLAW SALAD

serves 8

#1
Dissolve

    1 (6-ounce) package lemon gelatin

in

    1 cup hot water

Add

    1 cup ice water
    ¼ cup vinegar
    ½ tablespoon salt

Blend in

    1 cup mayonnaise

Chill until partially set. Then beat until fluffy. Fold in

    1½ cups shredded cabbage
    1½ cups shredded carrots

Pour into 1½-quart mold. Chill until firm. Unmold to serve.

CUCUMBER MOUSSE   *serves 12 to 15*

#1
Dissolve

    5 packages lime gelatin

in

    6 cups boiling water

Blend in with wire whisk

    1 cup sour cream

Let cool. Partially peel

    3 medium cucumbers

Grate them coarsely. Add cucumbers to gelatin mixture with

1 cup mayonnaise
3 tablespoons hot prepared horseradish
1 teaspoon salt
3 tablespoons cider vinegar
2 teaspoons grated onion

Pour into 3-quart mold and refrigerate overnight. Unmold to serve. This looks very attractive served surrounded with

tomato slices

the center filled with

marinated cucumber slices

DILLY BEANS *serves 6 to 8*

\#3
Cut and cook

6 to 8 cups fresh green beans

Rinse under cold water to stop cooking process. Season with

salt

While beans are cooling, combine

½ cup white vinegar
½ cup sugar
½ cup water
1 teaspoon dried dill weed

Mix and pour over beans. Marinate at least overnight. Serve chilled.

EGG AND AVOCADO SALAD
serves 10

Toss together

    3 ounces crumbled Roquefort cheese
    2 avocados, cut into strips and dipped in lemon juice
    1 head lettuce, shredded
    3 hard-cooked eggs, sliced

Toss with

    1 cup garlic-flavored French dressing

Note: Avocados must be dipped in lemon juice to keep them from turning dark.

GREEK SALAD
serves 8

Toss together and chill

    1 head lettuce, shredded
    1 cup chopped celery
    2 cucumbers, chopped
    2 small onions, sliced thin
    4 medium tomatoes, sliced
    1 green pepper, chopped

10 black olives, sliced
½ pound Feta cheese, crumbled

When ready to serve, toss again with

juice of 4 lemons
⅔ cup olive oil

Garnish with

1 can of sardines, drained
2 teaspoons oregano

Carry to picnic with lemon juice and olive oil separate; add those ingredients when ready to serve.

GUACAMOLE   *serves 6*

In Mexico, guacamole is served as a first course or as a salad. It is fine with corn chips, but even better and more authentic with warm tortillas on which it is spread. The tortillas are then rolled up.

Mash

3 avocados

Rinse, drain, and mince fine

1½ ounces canned hot chiles (like chiles serrano)

Combine the mashed avocado, and chiles with

> ⅔ cup coarsely chopped tomato
> 1 small onion, minced
> 1 sprig fresh coriander, minced

If not used immediately, set avocado pit in center of mixture; cover tightly and refrigerate. Serve with

> **warm tortillas or corn chips**

for a dip or as a salad.

GUACAMOLE SALAD   *serves 8 to 10*

Dice and combine

> 2 ripe avocados, dipped in lemon juice
> 4 hard-cooked eggs
> 3 tomatoes

Add

> ½ cup sliced, pimiento-stuffed olives
> 1 small onion, minced

Moisten with

> **French dressing**

Season to taste with

chili powder

Serve on lettuce topped with

3 **slices of crisp bacon, crumbled**

GUACAMOLE TOMATOES   *serves 8*

#1
Wash, core, and scoop pulp from

8 **small tomatoes**

Combine in a bowl and mash with potato masher

½ **cup tomato pulp**
1 **ripe avocado**
½ **teaspoon chili powder**
1 **tablespoon grated onion**
1 **tablespoon lemon juice**
½ **teaspoon salt**
¼ **teaspoon pepper**

Put mixture back into tomatoes. Refrigerate until well chilled—
at least 4 hours.

HONEY LIME SALAD   *serves 12*

#2
*The dressing may be prepared ahead; the salad greens cut up
and stored in plastic bag; the orange and onion cut up and
wrapped.*

Pour off most of the oil from a bottle of

oil and vinegar dressing

Combine ¾ cup of remaining dressing or use ¾ cup homemade oil and vinegar dressing (see below) with

> ¾ **cup lime juice**
> ¾ **cup honey**

Mix well and refrigerate. To serve, combine

> 12 **cups salad greens**
> 3 **cut-up oranges**
> 3 **medium onions, sliced into rings**
> 3 **avocados, diced**

Pour dressing over this mixture and toss. Top with

> 1 **box strawberries**

MARINATED GREEN BEANS

makes 1⅓ cups dressing—serves 8

#2
Place the following ingredients in a tightly covered container:

> 1 **cup olive oil**
> ⅓ **cup wine vinegar or lemon juice (or mixture of both)**
> 1 **teaspoon salt**
> ½ **teaspoon paprika**
> ¼ **teaspoon dry mustard**

1 teaspoon Worcestershire sauce
1 clove garlic

Chill mixture well. Remove garlic clove after standing one night. Before serving, shake vigorously until ingredients are well blended. Serve over

3 pounds crisply cooked green beans, chilled

MIXED BAG SALAD   *serves 12*

#2
Combine

2 (13- to 15-ounce) cans hearts of palm, drained and sliced
3 (10-ounce) packages frozen cut green beans, cooked and drained
1 (5- to 6-ounce) can pitted black olives, drained
1 (4-ounce) jar pimientos, drained and cut in julienne strips
1 (14-ounce) can artichoke hearts, drained
1 (3- or 4-ounce) jar marinated mushrooms

Pour over this mixture

1 (8-ounce) bottle oil and vinegar dressing or vinaigrette dressing (see p. 128)

Note: For proper flavor, vegetables must be marinated at least overnight.

MIXED VEGETABLE SALAD   *serves 6*

#1
Cook until just tender

>   1 (20-ounce) package frozen mixed vegetables

Drain thoroughly and mix with

>   1 teaspoon salt
>   1 (4-ounce) jar cocktail onions, drained
>   6 tablespoons mayonnaise
>   1 tablespoon fresh dill

Toss lightly and chill overnight. Serve on bed of watercress or lettuce.

ORANGE AND BLUE CHEESE   *serves 8*
SALAD

Toss together

>   1 small head romaine lettuce, torn up
>   2 oranges, peeled and sliced ½-inch thick
>   ½ cup sliced, pitted black olives
>   3 ounces blue cheese, crumbled

Combine for dressing

>   2 tablespoons lemon juice
>   6 tablespoons olive oil
>   salt and pepper to taste

When ready to serve, toss dressing with salad.

PRIZE WINNING MOLDED
POTATO SALAD

serves 8

#2
This recipe won Marian a trip to Europe.

Soften

1 envelope unflavored gelatin

in

¼ cup water

Heat

¾ cup pickle juice

Add to softened gelatin and stir until dissolved. Pour a thin layer of this mixture into 1½ quart mold. Chill until almost firm. Decorate using

carrot slices, black and green olives

Add remaining gelatin mixture to mixture of

4 cups diced, cooked potatoes
1 cup diced celery
½ cup diced onion
½ cup diced sweet pickle
4 hard-cooked eggs, chopped
1 cup mayonnaise
½ teaspoon salt

Stir well to blend. Spoon over gelatin in mold. Chill until firm. To serve, unmold.

RED CABBAGE FILLED WITH
COLE SLAW   *serves 8 to 10*

#2
Unusual serving piece.

Scoop center from

    1 large, solid head red cabbage

Shred the scooped out red cabbage and add to

    1 cup shredded white cabbage

Soak cabbage in ice water for 1 hour. Drain well. Mix with

    ½ cup mayonnaise
    1 tablespoon vinegar
    1 tablespoon olive oil
    1 tablespoon onion juice
    ¼ cup sugar
    ½ bunch parsley, chopped
    ½ cup sour cream

When ready to serve, fill cabbage head with cole slaw and serve
from it.

ROMAN SALAD

serves 6 to 8

#2
For dressing, combine in blender

    6 tablespoons olive oil
    1 tablespoon wine vinegar
    juice of 1 lemon
    4 anchovy fillets
    1 tablespoon Dijon mustard
    3 raw egg yolks
    2 tablespoons blue cheese
    2 tablespoons grated Parmesan cheese
    ½ teaspoon Worcestershire sauce
    1 clove garlic, crushed
    1 teaspoon salt
    ¼ teaspoon pepper

Cut into small cubes for croutons

    2 cups French bread

Toast the cubes, then pour over them

    4 tablespoons olive oil
    1 clove garlic, crushed

Let croutons stand in oil until ready to toss salad.
When ready to serve, toss together

    6 cups torn salad greens (romaine, escarole, Boston
      lettuce)
    croutons
    dressing

SALADE NIÇOISE   *serves 8*

#1
Dressing:
Combine, beat, and set aside

> 2 teaspoons Dijon mustard
> 2 tablespoons wine vinegar
> 1½ teaspoons salt
> 1 clove garlic, minced
> 6 tablespoons vegetable oil
> 6 tablespoons olive oil
> 1 teaspoon dried thyme
> dash of black pepper

Arrange for salad a careful design of the following ingredients

> 2 pounds green beans, cut and cooked just until tender
> 2 green peppers, thinly sliced in rounds
> 2 cups celery, sliced crosswise
> 1 pint cherry tomatoes
> 5 medium-sized potatoes, cooked, peeled, and sliced
> 3 (7-ounce) cans tuna fish, drained
> 1 (2-ounce) can flat anchovies, drained
> 10 pimiento-stuffed green olives
> 10 black olives, pitted
> 1 red onion, sliced to transparent circles
> ⅓ cup chopped fresh parsley
> ¼ cup chopped green onions
> 6 hard-cooked eggs, quartered

When ready to serve, toss salad with dressing. Carry dressing to picnic in plastic container; carry salad ingredients separately. Assemble when ready to serve.

SEA BREEZE SPINACH MOLD   *serves 8*

#2
Sprinkle

 2 envelopes unflavored gelatin

over

 ¼ cup cold water
 ¼ cup condensed beef broth (from 10½-ounce can)

in a blender container. Heat remaining beef broth to boiling.
Add to blender, cover, and blend until gelatin is dissolved.
Add.

 ¼ teaspoon salt
 2 tablespoons lemon juice
 1 cup sour cream

Blend again and add

 ¼ cup onion

Blend until onion is chopped. Add

 1 (10-ounce) package frozen chopped spinach, thawed
 4 hard-cooked eggs, quartered

Blend until eggs are coarsely chopped. Stir in

 ½ pound bacon, crisply cooked and crumbled

Turn into 6-cup mold. Chill until firm. Unmold and garnish with

 cherry tomatoes

SPICED APRICOT MOLD   *serves 8*

#2
Drain, but reserve syrup from

> 1 (1-pound) can unpeeled apricot halves
> 1 (8¾-ounce) can pineapple tidbits

Combine syrups with

> 2 tablespoons vinegar
> 1 teaspoon whole cloves
> 4 (1-inch) sticks cinnamon

Boil for 10 minutes, then strain and add enough hot water to make 2 cups liquid. Pour the hot liquid over

> 1 (3-ounce) package orange gelatin

Stir to dissolve. Chill until partially set, then fold in fruits and pour into 1½-quart mold. Chill until firm. Dissolve

> 1 (3-ounce) package orange gelatin

in

> ¾ cup boiling water

Add

> ¾ cup apricot nectar

Chill until partially set. Whip until fluffy. Swirl in

> ½ cup sour cream

Spoon over first chilled layer and refrigerate until firm. Unmold to serve.

STRAWBERRY CRANBERRY MOLD *serves 8 to 10*

#1
Drain and reserve juice from

    1 (8-ounce) can crushed pineapple

Defrost, drain, and reserve juice from

    1 (10-ounce) package frozen strawberries

Add to reserved juices enough water to make 2 cups liquid. Dissolve

    2 (3-ounce) packages strawberry gelatin

in

    2 cups boiling water

Then add fruit liquid. Chill slightly; then fold in

    strawberries
    crushed pineapple
    1 (1-pound) can whole cranberry sauce

Pour into lightly greased 1½-quart mold. Chill until firm. Unmold to serve.

STUFFED MUSHROOM CAPS *makes 2 dozen*

#1
Remove stems from

1 pound large mushrooms

Chop stems. Sauté caps for 5 minutes in

3 tablespoons butter

Remove from pan. In remaining butter in same pan, sauté

½ cup chopped stems

Combine stems with

4 ounces blue cheese
4 teaspoons light cream
2 tablespoons chopped chives

Fill caps with mixture. Chill.

THREE BEAN SALAD *serves 6*

#2
As good a version of this old stand-by as you'll find anywhere.

In large bowl combine

1 (1-pound) can kidney beans, drained and washed
1 (1-pound) can whole string beans, drained and washed

1 (1-pound) can cut wax beans, drained and washed
2 cups diced celery
1 (6-ounce) can sliced mushrooms, drained
½ cup chopped onion
½ cup chopped green pepper

Combine

½ cup vinegar
2 tablespoons olive oil
¼ cup sugar
1 teaspoon nutmeg
½ teaspoon salt
⅛ teaspoon freshly ground black pepper

Pour over vegetables. Toss well and refrigerate overnight.

TOMATO CHEESE SALAD   *serves 8*

#2
Combine

⅔ cup olive oil
¼ cup tarragon vinegar
2 cloves garlic, minced or pressed
4 ounces blue cheese, crumbled
salt and pepper

Refrigerate. To serve, slice

8 tomatoes

Combine with dressing and season to taste.

VEGETABLE ANTIPASTO   *serves 6*

#2
Cook according to package directions

> 1 (10-ounce) package frozen artichoke hearts

Drain thoroughly.
Wash and dry

> 2 cups small-to-medium mushrooms

Add to artichokes in small bowl. Pour over them

> 1 cup herb and garlic dressing, homemade or bottled

Chill overnight. To serve, drain off marinade and combine
vegetables with

> 2 tomatoes, cut into eighths

VEGETABLE SALAD   *serves 8*

#1
Toss together

> 4 cooked potatoes, peeled and sliced
> 2 (10-ounce) packages frozen cut green beans, cooked
>   and drained
> 2 (10-ounce) packages frozen peas, cooked and drained
> herbed mayonnaise (see p. 149)

Line a large salad bowl with

leaves of romaine lettuce

Place vegetables in center. Surround with

1 (1-pound) can asparagus, drained
3 large ripe tomatoes, quartered
4 hard-cooked eggs, sliced lengthwise

Garnish salad with

1 (2-ounce) can flat anchovy fillets, drained
green olives
black olives
capers
parsley

Herbed Mayonnaise:

Place in blender

¼ clove garlic
1 tablespoon dried dill weed
1 tablespoon chopped chives
1 egg
1 teaspoon salt
1 teaspoon dry mustard
2 tablespoons wine vinegar
¼ cup olive oil

Cover blender and turn motor to low speed. Add in a steady stream

¾ cup more olive oil

Turn off motor when last drop of oil has been added.

To serve at picnic, carry dressing in covered plastic jar in insulated container to keep cold. Carry salad ingredients separately and assemble when ready to serve.

WESTERN TOSS   *serves 8*

Toss and let stand 1 hour

    ½ head iceberg lettuce, shredded
    ½ pound fresh mushrooms, sliced
    ⅓ cup salad oil
    3 tablespoons wine vinegar
    1 teaspoon salt
    1 teaspoon dried basil or 3 teaspoons fresh
    ½ teaspoon lemon-pepper

When ready to serve toss in

    ½ head more lettuce, shredded
    ¾ cup mild Cheddar cheese, cubed
    1 pint cherry tomatoes, halved

ZUCCHINI SALAD   *serves 8*

Combine
    3 heads lettuce (Boston, endive, romaine or similar)
    1 zucchini, washed and sliced thinly
    ½ pint cherry tomatoes, halved
    ¼ pound fresh mushrooms, sliced

    ½ Bermuda onion, thinly sliced or 1 bunch green
        onions, sliced
    1 avocado, thinly sliced

#2
For dressing, combine

    juice of two lemons
    ⅔ cup olive oil
    2 tablespoons wine vinegar
    salt and freshly ground black pepper to taste
    1 teaspoon Dijon mustard
    pinch of sugar (optional)
    1 teaspoon fresh dill
    ¼ teaspoon fresh tarragon
    ½ teaspoon fresh basil

Pour dressing over salad and toss well. Serve.

Breads

ARABIC OR SYRIAN BREAD

serves 8

#1
Split in half

2 round Syrian breads

Spread each circle with

butter

Cut each circle into eighths. Sprinkle liberally with

    garlic salt
    sesame seeds

Place on cookie sheet. Bake at 300° for 10 minutes, until crisp.

BETSY'S HERB BREAD

serves 8

❋ #2
From a famous Connecticut kitchen.

Soften

    ½ cup butter

Add to butter and mix well

    2 tablespoons chopped parsley
    1 clove garlic, crushed
    ¼ teaspoon ground coriander
    1 teaspoon ginger
    ½ teaspoon celery seed

Cut into 1-inch slices, but not quite through

    1 (18-inch) loaf French or Italian bread

Butter all available spaces. Wrap in foil and refrigerate or freeze until ready to use. Return to room temperature; then heat at 400° for 10 to 15 minutes.

CHEESE BUTTERMILK BREAD
serves 8

* #2
Combine

    1½ cups buttermilk
     1 egg
     3 cups biscuit mix
     2 tablespoons sugar

Beat 1 minute to blend thoroughly. Gently stir in

    1 cup (about ¼ pound) grated Swiss cheese
    1 cup sliced, pimiento-stuffed olives
   ¾ cup chopped walnuts

Spoon into well-greased 9-by-5-by-3-inch loaf pan and bake at 350° 50 to 55 minutes. (A crack along top of loaf usually occurs.) Cool 5 minutes before removing from pan. Continue cooling on wire rack. Freeze or refrigerate as desired. Return to room temperature to serve.
Carry to picnic site wrapped in foil.

CHEESE RING LOAF
serves 6

❁

Heavily grease a 5½-cup ring mold.
Arrange

    1 (8-ounce) package refrigerated butterflake rolls

around bottom of ring mold, pressing to cover base completely.
Sprinkle with

½ package (4 ounces) grated Cheddar cheese

Top with

1 (8-ounce) package refrigerated butterflake rolls

and sprinkle with remainder of Cheddar cheese. Brush top with

butter

Bake at 350° for 35 to 40 minutes, until golden brown and cheese
is melted. Turn out on wire rack. Remove from pan. Or bake for
15 minutes and freeze. To serve, return to room temperature, and
bake at 350° 20 to 30 minutes longer. Serve warm.

FARMHOUSE BREAD

serves 6

#2
Grease a 9-by-5-by-3-inch loaf pan very well. Open

2 (8-ounce) cans refrigerated biscuits

Spread all but two of these rolls with contents of

1 (4-ounce) can chicken spread

Arrange biscuits, standing them on edge, in the loaf pan, using
two plain ones at each end. Brush loaf with mixture of

1 egg yolk
1 tablespoon water

Bake at 375° for 30 minutes. Refrigerate, if desired. To serve, reheat until warm through.

FRENCH BREAD   *serves 8*

＊#1
Cut almost through into 1-inch slices

1 loaf brown-and-serve French bread

Cream together

3 tablespoons butter
½ medium-sized onion, minced
1 tablespoon poppy seeds
1½ tablespoons prepared mustard

Spread butter mixture on all cut surfaces. Insert in each cut

a 2½-inch-square slice of Swiss cheese (use ¼ pound)

Spread remaining butter on top. To prepare ahead, refrigerate or freeze at this point. When ready to serve, return to room temperature. Bake at 375° for 20 minutes. To carry to picnic, wrap in heavy duty aluminum foil while still warm. Reheat on top of grill.

HERB BREAD

* #1
Handy to have in the freezer all the time.

Blend together

> ½ cup butter, softened
> 1 teaspoon parsley
> ½ teaspoon garlic powder
> ½ teaspoon dried basil or dill weed

Spread mixture on

> 1 loaf very thinly sliced white bread

Cut bread slices into triangular halves and, when ready to serve, arrange pinwheel fashion on platter.

HERB BREAD STICKS

* #1
Cut into 1-by-5-inch sticks

> 1 loaf unsliced white bread

In large shallow pan, melt

> ½ cup butter

Roll each stick in melted butter, then sprinkle with

garlic salt
onion salt
celery salt
Parmesan cheese
sesame seeds
poppy seeds

(A good combination is Parmesan cheese and garlic.) Refrigerate or freeze. When ready to serve, return to room temperature. Arrange in buttered baking pan and bake at 375° for 20 to 25 minutes, turning occasionally to brown all sides. Serve warm.

INDIVIDUAL YORKSHIRE PUDDINGS

serves 8

#1
Sift together

⅔ cup flour
⅔ teaspoon salt

Cut in

2 teaspoons shortening

Add

1 egg
⅔ cup milk

Beat at high speed for 10 minutes. Chill thoroughly in refrigerator. Place empty muffin tins in 425° oven until very hot. Pour into each of 8 cups

1 teaspoon melted shortening (use about 3 tablespoons total)

Fill cups ½ full with batter. Bake at 425° for 30 minutes. These may be prepared ahead and reheated in 350° oven for 10 minutes.

ONION CHEESE BREAD

#1
Split in half, but not all the way through

16 French baguettes (small narrow French rolls) *

Mix to consistency of softened butter

¾ cup mayonnaise
¾ cup freshly grated Parmesan cheese

Mix in

4 teaspoons finely chopped onion

Spread the cut side of the rolls with this mixture. Close rolls up and refrigerate. When ready to serve, return to room temperature and heat at 350° for 5 to 7 minutes, until rolls are hot and mixture is melted. Can be heated on the grill, too, wrapped in foil.

* If baguettes are not available, use some other small crusty roll.

ONION HERB RING

serves 8

* #1
Combine and set aside for 10 minutes

¼ **cup water**
¼ **cup dried minced or chopped onion**

Combine yeast from

1 **(13 ¾-ounce) package hot roll mix**

with

¾ **cup warm water**

Stir until yeast is dissolved. Combine and add

onion
1 **egg, slightly beaten**
¾ **teaspoon dried marjoram**
¾ **teaspoon dried thyme**
½ **teaspoon dried basil**
⅛ **teaspoon salt**

Stir in roll mix. Blend well. Cover and let rise in warm place until dough doubles in bulk (45 to 50 minutes). Punch down. Shape into 6 balls about 2½ inches in diameter. Place balls side by side in a well-greased 1½-quart ring mold. Set in warm place to rise again until double in bulk. Bake at 350° for 30 to 35 minutes. Refrigerate or freeze. To carry to picnic, slice and butter, reheat and wrap in foil while still hot.

ORANGE CRANBERRY MUFFINS   *makes 12*

* #1
Cream

> ¼ cup butter
> ⅓ cup sugar

Beat in

> 2 large eggs

Sift together

> 2 cups flour
> 1 tablespoon baking powder
> ½ teaspoon salt

Add flour to creamed mixture alternately with

> 1½ teaspoons grated orange rind
> ⅔ cup orange juice

Fill 12 buttered muffin tins ⅓ full. Add to each

> 1 teaspoon whole cranberry sauce, drained

Fill with batter until ⅔ full. Bake at 400° for 20 minutes. Freeze if desired. To serve, return to room temperature and reheat in muffin tins.
Note: Carry muffins in tins to picnic and reheat on grill.

ORANGE PECAN BREAD   *serves 8*

*#2
Mix together quickly (don't worry about lumps)

- 1 cup sugar
- 1 egg
- 2 tablespoons butter
- 2 tablespoons grated orange rind
- ¾ cup orange juice
- 2 cups flour
- 1 teaspoon baking powder
- ½ teaspoon baking soda
- 1 teaspoon salt

Add to batter

- ½ cup dates, halved
- ½ cup chopped pecans

Pour into buttered 9-by-5-by-3-inch loaf pan and bake at 350° for 50 minutes. Cool thoroughly. Freeze if desired. Return to room temperature and serve sliced very thin. Spread slices with

whipped cream cheese

Cakes
and Pies

ANITA'S COFFEECAKE

serves 8

*#1
Thoroughly blend

    8 ounces cream cheese, softened
    ½ cup butter
    1¼ cups sugar

Add

    2 eggs
    ¼ cup milk
    1 teaspoon vanilla

Add and mix well

> 2 cups sifted flour
> 1 teaspoon baking powder
> ½ teaspoon baking soda
> ¼ teaspoon salt

Pour half of this mixture into greased and floured 9-by13-inch pan. Cover with

> 1 (12-ounce) jar apricot preserves

Dot with remaining batter. Bake at 350° for 35 to 40 minutes. Prepare topping by combining

> 2 cups shredded coconut
> ⅔ cup packed brown sugar
> 1 teaspoon cinnamon
> ⅓ cup melted butter

Spread topping over hot cake. Broil 3 to 4 minutes until golden. Watch carefully as it may burn easily.

APRICOT MARZIPAN TART   *serves 8*

#1
Ever so beautiful.

Mix together with fingertips until creamy

> 2 cups flour
> ¾ cup butter at room temperature

    2 egg yolks
    2 tablespoons sugar

Sprinkle with

    1½ tablespoons ice water

Knead all together. Chill until firm enough to roll (about 30 minutes). Roll between sheets of wax paper to ⅛-inch thickness. Place in a 10-inch flan ring or 10-inch springform pan and bake for 10 minutes at 350°.
For filling, cream together

    ½ cup sweet butter
    8 ounces almond paste

Beat in

    2 eggs

Blend in

    2 teaspoons flour
    2 tablespoons brandy

Smooth almond mixture into shell. Set on lowest rack in oven and bake for 45 minutes at 350°. Remove to cooling rack. Arrange on top of filling, covering completely,

    1 (29-ounce) can apricot halves, well drained

For glaze, melt together in saucepan

    ¾ cup apricot preserves
    2 tablespoons brandy

Brush glaze over entire top of tart. Cool.

BLUEBERRY PIE WITH ORANGE NUT CRUST

serves 8

---

*#1
A new version of a classic.

Crust:

Mix in bowl

>   2 cups flour
> ¼ teaspoon salt
>   2 teaspoons sugar

Cut in

> ¾ cup shortening

Add

> 1 teaspoon grated orange rind
> ⅓ cup finely chopped walnuts or pecans

Add, one at a time,

> 5 tablespoons ice water

Form dough with hands. Roll into ball and refrigerate 1 hour. Roll out half the pastry to line a 9-inch pie plate.

Filling:

Mix together and pour into pastry

    4 cups fresh blueberries
    1 cup sugar
    ¼ cup cornstarch
    ½ teaspoon nutmeg

Dot with

    2 tablespoons butter

Roll out remaining pastry for top crust. Cut a few slits in top of pie. Freeze if desired. Return to room temperature and bake at 375° for 1 hour. Cool on rack. When cool, sprinkle with

    confectioners' sugar

BROWNIE TORTE
serves 8

*#1
Melt together in top of double boiler

    ½ cup butter
    2 squares unsweetened chocolate

Cream

    1 cup sugar
    2 eggs

Combine butter and chocolate with eggs and sugar and add

    2 teaspoons vanilla
    ½ cup flour
    ½ cup chopped walnuts

Spread batter in greased 10-by-15-inch jelly roll pan and bake at 400° for 10 to 12 minutes. Cool on wire rack. When cool, cut into 3 oblongs (5-by-10-inches) and remove from pan. Spread on 2 layers

thin layer raspberry jam
Fudge Frosting (see below)

Place layers on top of each other, with unfrosted layer on top. Frost top layer with additional frosting and decorate with more nuts.

Fudge Frosting:

Melt in top of double boiler

4 ounces sweet chocolate

Combine melted chocolate with

½ cup sour cream

CHOCOLATE NUT LOAVES   *makes 2 loaves*

* #2
Sift together

2½ cups sifted cake flour
1 teaspoon baking soda
1 teaspoon salt

Cream

    1 cup vegetable shortening

Gradually add

    2 cups sugar

Cream until light and fluffy. Add, one at a time, beating thoroughly after each addition

    5 eggs

Blend in

    3 squares unsweetened chocolate, melted

Then alternately add flour mixture with

    1⅓ cups buttermilk or sour milk

Beat after each addition until smooth. Blend in

    2 teaspoons vanilla
    1 cup finely chopped nuts

Pour into two 9-by-5-by-3-inch loaf pans lined on bottom with wax paper. Bake at 350° about 1 hour. Cool and freeze, if desired. Defrost to serve.
Note: One loaf will serve 6.

DEVIL'S FOOD CAKE

serves 12

* #1
Light, delectable, and topped with rich frosting.

Cream together until light and fluffy

> 1 (1-pound) box light brown sugar
> ¾ cup butter
> 3 eggs
> 2 teaspoons vanilla

Stir in

> 3 squares unsweetened chocolate, melted

Sift together

> 2¼ cups sifted cake flour
> ¾ teaspoon salt
> 2 teaspoons baking soda

Add dry ingredients alternately to creamed mixture with

> ½ cup milk (soured with 1 teaspoon vinegar)

Add

> 1 cup boiling water

(batter will be thin) and pour into 9-by-13-inch pan that has been lined with greased wax paper. Bake at 350° for 35 minutes or until cake tests done. Cool for 10 minutes on wire rack before removing from pan. Frost with Chocolate Frosting when cooled.

Chocolate Frosting:

Cream together

>   1 (1-pound) box confectioners' sugar
>   4 tablespoons butter
>   2 teaspoons vanilla
>   1 egg
>   4 squares unsweetened chocolate, melted
>   pinch of salt

Add no more than

>   ¼ cup hot water

slowly, until frosting is of correct spreading consistency. Beat until fluffy. Swirl on cooled cake.

DUNDEE CAKE   *serves 8*

#7
Don't even attempt to cut this cake until it has rested a few days in a cool place.

Beat until fluffy

>   1 cup butter

Cream until light with

>   ⅔ cup sugar

One at a time, add

4 eggs

Beat well after each addition. Stir in

¼ cup Scotch whiskey or apple cider

Mixture may look curdled, but it doesn't matter. Sift together

2¼ cups sifted flour
1 teaspoon baking powder
½ teaspoon salt

Beat into mixture for about 4 minutes, until smooth. Fold in

1 cup chopped, mixed, candied fruits
1 cup currants or seedless raisins
1 cup finely chopped pecans

Pour batter into greased and floured 8-inch spring form pan. Bake at 325° for 45 minutes to 1 hour or until firm to the touch. Cool in pan 10 minutes; then remove sides and cool completely. Dip cheesecloth into

Scotch or apple cider

and wring out. Wrap cake in cloth and then wrap in foil or place in airtight tin box. Store in cool place for several days before cutting into very thin slices.

GLAZED CHOCOLATE CHIP CAKE

*#1
Sift together

    2¼ cups sifted cake flour
      1 cup sugar
      2 teaspoons baking powder
      1 teaspoon salt

Add and beat 2 minutes

      ½ cup butter or margarine
      1 teaspoon vanilla
      5 egg yolks
      ½ cup milk

Add and beat 2 more minutes

      ¼ cup milk

Grate

      2 squares unsweetened chocolate

Add

      ½ cup chopped pecans

and the chocolate to the batter. Pour mixture into greased and floured 9-by-5-by-3-inch loaf pan and bake at 350° for 60 to 70 minutes. Cool in pan.
Mix together

      ½ cup orange juice
      1 cup confectioner's sugar

Spoon this mixture over top of warm cake. Pierce top surface of cake with fork to allow glaze to penetrate. Freeze if desired after cake is cool.

ITALIAN CHEESE PIE

serves 8

***#1**
Beat well

>   3 egg yolks

Add and beat

>   ½ cup sugar

Then beat in

>   1 pound ricotta cheese
>   ½ teaspoon vanilla

Beat stiff

>   3 egg whites
>   4 tablespoons sugar

Fold whites into yolk mixture. Pour into

>   **unbaked 9-inch pie shell**

Make lattice of crust strips on top. Dot strips with

>   **butter**

Bake at 400° for 30 minutes. Leave in oven to cool. When cooled,
remove from oven and sprinkle top with

>   **confectioners' sugar**

KATAIFI

serves 8

#1
A good American adaptation.

Place in bottom of 8-inch square baking dish

    6 pieces shredded wheat (½ 10-ounce box)

which have been dipped in

    1 cup milk

Combine for filling

    1½ cups chopped walnuts
    1½ cups butter, melted
    ½ cup sugar
    1 egg
    1 teaspoon cinnamon

Pour filling over bottom layer. Cover with

    6 more pieces shredded wheat

Bake at 350° for 30 minutes. Remove from oven and cool on wire rack. Meanwhile combine and bring to a boil

    ½ pound sugar
    1½ cups water
    juice and rind of 1 orange
    a few whole cloves

Strain syrup and pour hot over cooled baked Kataifi. Let cool. Cut into serving pieces.

LEMON CREAM TORTE

serves 8

#1
Meringue:

Beat until foamy

>3 **egg whites**

Add

>¼ **teaspoon salt**
>¼ **teaspoon cream of tartar**

Beat until soft peaks form. Gradually beat in

>¾ **cup sugar**

Beat until stiff. Spread on bottom and sides of buttered 9-inch spring form pan. Bake at 300° for 50 minutes. Cool in oven.

Lemon Cream:

Beat together in top of double boiler

>3 **egg yolks**
>1 **whole egg**

Mix in

>¾ **cup sugar**
>¼ **cup lemon juice**
>1½ **teaspoons grated lemon rind**
>3 **tablespoons butter**

Cook over hot water, stirring, until thick. Remove from heat and cool.

Assembly:

Spread bottom of meringue with

    ½ **cup heavy cream, whipped**

Top with lemon cream. Chill. At serving time, cover top of torte completely with

    1 **pint whole fresh strawberries, the larger the better**

PEACHY COCOA TORTE   *serves 8 to 10*

*#1
Combine

    1⅓ **cups flour**
     1 **teaspoon baking powder**
    ⅓ **cup sugar**

Cut in

    ½ **cup butter or margarine**

until mixture is crumbly. Stir in

    1 **egg, slightly beaten**

Press dough evenly on bottom and sides of 9-inch layer cake pan with or without removable bottom. Spread

½ cup peach jam (from 12-ounce jar)

over the dough. Chill.
Cream

½ cup butter or margarine
½ cup instant cocoa mix
3 tablespoons sugar

Blend in

½ teaspoon almond extract
1 cup blanched almonds, finely chopped

Add, one at a time, beating well after each addition

2 eggs

Spoon mixture over peach jam in cake pan. Bake at 350° about
50 minutes. Thoroughly cool torte in pan. Remove.
Combine

1 (1-pound) can sliced peaches, well drained
remainder of peach jam

Heat until jam melts and brush glaze over top of torte. Refrigerate
or freeze.

PRALINE CAKE

serves 12

#1
Sift together and set aside

    2 cups sifted cake flour
    2 teaspoons baking powder
    ¼ teaspoon salt

Cream

    ⅔ cup butter or margarine

Add and cream thoroughly

    1⅓ cups sugar

Add and beat well

    3 egg yolks

Add dry ingredients to creamed mixture alternately with

    ⅔ cup milk
    1 teaspoon vanilla

Fold in

    3 egg whites, stiffly beaten

Pour into greased and floured 9-by-13-inch baking pan. Level batter and bake at 350° for about 25 minutes. While cake is baking, melt

    ⅓ cup butter or margarine

Add, and blend well,

    ½ cup brown sugar

Mix in

¼ cup milk
dash of salt
½ teaspoon vanilla
1 cup shredded coconut
½ cup chopped pecans

When cake tests done, spread topping evenly over cake. Place under broiler and heat until top bubbles and toasts lightly.

RHUBARB AND STRAWBERRY PIE   *serves 8*

*#1
We wait all year for the rhubarb season just for this recipe.

Combine

2 cups 1-inch-long pieces fresh rhubarb
1 pint strawberries, hulled and quartered if large

Place in

9-inch unbaked pie shell

Combine and mix well

1¼ cups sugar
3 tablespoons flour
½ teaspoon nutmeg

Cut in

1 tablespoon butter

Beat in

    2 eggs

Pour this mixture over fruit. Arrange a lattice crust on top of pie. Freeze at this point if desired. To bake, return to room temperature and place in an oven preheated to 400°. Immediately lower heat to 350°. Bake about 1 hour, until pastry is done.

SPICY SPONGE CAKE   *serves 8*

* #1
Beat well

    6 egg yolks

Gradually add, beating

    ¾ cup sugar

Add and beat until all sugar is dissolved

    ¼ cup orange juice
    ¼ cup water
    ½ teaspoon vanilla

Sift together and add all at once

    1½ cups cake flour
    1 teaspoon baking powder
    ½ teaspoon cinnamon
    ¼ teaspoon nutmeg
    ¼ teaspoon allspice

Beat until just blended. Beat until stiff

> 6 egg whites

Gradually beat in

> ¾ cup sugar
> ¼ teaspoon salt

Fold whites into batter. Bake in ungreased 10-inch tube pan for 1 hour at 325°. Hang upside down to cool.

TIPSY DELIGHT

*#1
Break into pieces

> 2 cups pecans

Measure

> 1½ cups sifted flour

Sift twice more. Mix ½ cup flour with nuts and

> ½ pound seedless raisins

To remaining flour, add

> 1 teaspoon baking powder

Sift again. Cream

½ cup butter
1 cup plus 2 teaspoons sugar

Add, one at a time,

3 egg yolks

Beat until smooth and lemon-colored
Soak at least 10 minutes

2 teaspoons nutmeg

in

½ cup bourbon

Add flour and bourbon to butter mixture alternately, beating as batter is being blended. Slowly fold in raisins and nuts. Beat until stiff

3 egg whites
few grains of salt

Fold stiffly beaten whites into cake batter. Grease 9-inch tube pan and line bottom with wax paper. Bake at 325° for 1¼ hours. Let stand in pan 30 minutes before removing. Cake will crack.

Cookies and Small Cakes

APPLESAUCE SHORTCAKE SQUARES

makes 24 bars

*#1
Combine with pastry blender or fork

    ½ **cup softened butter or margarine**
    ½ **cup brown sugar**
    1 **cup flour**

Work until fine and crumbly. Press into 9-by-9-by-2-inch baking pan. Bake at 350° for 10 to 15 minutes or until golden brown. Remove from oven. Meanwhile combine

 1¼ cups canned applesauce
  2 tablespoons brown sugar
  1 tablespoon cornstarch
  1 teaspoon lemon juice
 ½ teaspoon grated lemon rind
 ¼ teaspoon salt
 ¼ teaspoon cinnamon

Cook 15 minutes, stirring occasionally. Add

 ½ cup chopped walnuts

Cool slightly and spread over pastry in pan. Combine

 1 beaten egg
 1 cup shredded coconut

Spread over applesauce mixture. Return to oven and bake 25 minutes. Cool thoroughly and cut into bars. Freeze if desired. To serve, return to room temperature.
Note: Carry to picnic site in baking pan covered with foil.

DELICE CHEESE BARS   *makes 16 large bars*

#2
From the Delice Pastry Shop in Aspen, Colorado. Fantastic!

Beat until light and creamy

½ cup butter
2 teaspoons sugar
2 tablespoons milk
½ teaspoon lemon rind
dash of salt

Mix in

1 cup plus 2 tablespoons cake flour

Blend well with fingers. Pat into ungreased 9-by-9-inch baking pan.
Blend together

1 pound cream cheese
1 cup granulated sugar
1 egg
1 teaspoon lemon rind
dash of salt

Beat well and stir in

1 cup chopped almonds

Pour over unbaked crust and bake at 300° for 1 hour and 10 minutes. Remove from oven. Combine

1 cup confectioners' sugar
1 tablespoon water
1 teaspoon cinnamon

Spread over hot cake. Cool cake, then refrigerate. Cut into bars only when thoroughly chilled.

FILLED MARZIPAN COOKIES

3 dozen

===

*#3
Cream together

> ½ cup butter
> ¼ cup sugar

Add

> 1 egg yolk
> 3 tablespoons almond paste

Blend in

> 1½ cups sifted cake flour

Chill. Roll on lightly floured cloth to ¼-inch thickness and cut into rounds about the size of a silver dollar. Arrange on greased cookie sheets. Work together with fingers

> 1 cup almond paste
> 1 egg white

Force almond paste mixture through small pastry tube to form circle in center of each cookie. Fill circles with

> **raspberry jam**

Bake at 350° for 15 minutes.

HELLO DOLLYS

*#3
*Somewhere in the dim dark past is a story about a southern ladies'
club naming these for Carol Channing when she came to town.*

Melt in a 9-by-9 inch pan

    ½ cup butter

Mix in

    1 cup graham cracker crumbs

Sprinkle with

    1 (6-ounce) package chocolate chips
    1 cup flaked coconut
    1 cup chopped pecans

Pour over this

    1 can sweetened condensed milk

Bake at 350° for 30 minutes. Cool and cut into 1-inch squares.
Freeze, if desired. To serve, return to room temperature.

LEMON CURD TARTS   *makes 2½ dozen*

#3
Beat until very light

3 small eggs

Combine them over hot water with

4 tablespoons butter
1 cup sugar
juice of 1½ lemons
grated rind of 1 lemon

Cook, stirring occasionally, until thick. Refrigerate. To serve, fill

miniature store-bought patty shells

with mixture, no more than an hour before serving. Carry lemon curd to picnic site in plastic jar in insulated container. Carry tarts separately.

MERINGUE COOKIES

makes 4 to 5 dozen

#3
Stiffly beat

4 egg whites

Gradually add

2 cups sugar

beating all the time until mixture is stiff and glossy. Add

4 cups corn flakes
4 cups chopped walnuts

Drop by tablespoonfuls on lightly greased aluminum foil on cookie sheets and flatten slightly. Bake at 325° 15 to 18 minutes, until pale golden.

Keep well wrapped in tightly covered container.

Note: Coconut or other nuts may be substituted for walnuts.

MOLASSES CHEWIES

makes 5 dozen

* #3

Cream together

> 1 cup white sugar
> 1 cup light brown sugar
> 1 cup butter

Add and beat well

> 2 eggs
> 2 teaspoons vanilla
> ¼ cup molasses

Sift together and stir in

> 4 cups flour
> 1 teaspoon salt
> 1½ teaspoons baking soda

Stir in

> 1 cup flaked coconut

Shape into small balls and place on greased cookie sheets about 3 inches apart. Bake at 375° for 10 to 12 minutes.

OATMEAL WAFERS   *makes about 4 dozen*

*#3
Esther Peterson, a fabulous baker, is the source for these.

Melt

> ½ cup butter

Stir in

> ¾ cup sugar
> 1 teaspoon cinnamon
> 1 cup quick-cooking oatmeal
> 2 tablespoons flour
> 1 teaspoon baking powder
> 1 egg

Mix well. Butter and flour cookie sheets (as many as you have.)
Drop batter from teaspoon onto cookie sheets, 3 inches apart.
Bake at 375° about 6 to 8 minutes, until golden brown.
Let stand 1 to 2 minutes before removing. Then remove quickly
from cookie sheet with sharp knife and curve over broom handle
(washed!) to cool. Store in covered box to keep crisp, or freeze.
These are very fragile.
Note: If they cool too quickly to be shaped, return to oven for a
minute or less, to soften.

ORANGE MARMALADE BARS   *makes 36*

*#1
Don't be surprised; these are very crumbly.

Chop

    2 cups pitted prunes

Combine prunes with

    ½ cup water
    1 (12-ounce) jar orange marmalade
    ¼ teaspoon salt

Bring to boil and simmer 10 minutes, stirring occasionally; cool. In large bowl, combine

    2 cups quick rolled oats
  1¾ cups flour
    ¾ teaspoon salt
    ½ teaspoon baking soda
    1 cup brown sugar

Mix well. Add

    ½ cup shortening
    ½ cup butter or margarine

Mix until evenly distributed in dry ingredients. Divide in half. Pack half into bottom of 9-inch square baking pan. Spread with marmalade filling. Pat remaining oatmeal mixture on top. Bake at 350° 45 to 50 minutes. Cool in pan on wire rack. Cut into bars 1-by-2 inches.

Freeze, if desired.

Note: Carry to picnic site in baking pan, wrapped in aluminum foil.

PAT'S CHOCOROON CUPCAKES   *makes 22*

*#2
President of New Haven Wellesley Club, Pat Cavanagh, gets credit for these.

Melt in top of double boiler

> 4 squares semi-sweet chocolate
> 1 cup butter

Stir in until well coated

> 1½ cups chopped walnuts or pecans

Combine in a bowl, but do not beat,

> 1¾ cups sugar
> 1 cup flour
> 4 eggs
> 1 teaspoon vanilla

Add chocolate-nut mixture and mix, but do not beat. Fill paper-lined cupcake tins ⅔ full. Bake at 325° for 35 minutes. These may also be made in miniature muffin tins. If so, they will need to bake for 25 minutes and will make 5 dozen.

PECAN TARTS   *makes 2 dozen*

*#2
Blend

> 1 (3-ounce) package cream cheese, softened
> ½ cup butter, softened

Stir in

> 1 cup sifted flour

Form into ball. Cover with wax paper and chill in refrigerator 1 hour. Shape mixture into 2 dozen 1-inch balls and press into small muffin tins, forming small cups.
Combine

> 1 egg
> ¾ cup brown sugar
> 1 teaspoon softened butter
> 1 teaspoon vanilla
> dash of salt
> ⅓ cup finely chopped pecans

Mix well and fill each pastry cup with a teaspoon of the mixture. Top with

> ⅓ cup finely chopped pecans

Bake at 325° for 25 minutes. Freeze, if desired. Serve at room temperature.

THREE D BROWNIES   *makes about 2½ dozen*

* #1
Melt together

> 4 squares unsweetened chocolate
> 1 cup butter

Add this to

    2 cups sugar

Beat lightly and add to mixture

    4 eggs

Beat well and add

    1 cup flour
    1 teaspoon vanilla
    ½ teaspoon salt
    1 cup broken nutmeats

Mix well and pour into greased 9-by-13-inch baking pan. Bake at
325° for 30 to 35 minutes. When brownies are cool spread with
frosting made as follows:
Combine

    3 cups confectioners' sugar
    2 tablespoons butter, softened

Add enough

    cream

to make spreading consistency. When frosting is set, ice brownies.
Melt

    4 squares semi-sweet chocolate
    2 tablespoons butter

Spread this over first icing. Freeze or refrigerate, if desired. Serve
at room temperature, cut into small bars.

Cold
Desserts

BLOSSIE'S SPECIAL

serves 8

*#3
Butter an 8-by-8-inch pan. Crush

   ½ **pound vanilla wafers**

Cover the bottom of the pan with half the crumbs. Cream

   ¾ **cup butter**

with

1 pound confectioners' sugar

Drain

1 (4-ounce) can crushed pineapple

Stir ⅔ of pineapple into creamed mixture. Add and mix well

2 eggs at room temperature

Stir in

6 tablespoons brandy

Pour ½ this filling mixture over the crumbs in the pan. Top with remaining crumbs, then rest of filling. Cover with

1 pint heavy cream, whipped

and spoon on remaining pineapple. Cover and refrigerate at least overnight. Freeze, if desired.

To serve, if frozen, defrost in refrigerator. Cut pieces right from pan.

CARAMEL FLAN   *serves 8*

#1
Cook over medium heat, stirring until sugar caramelizes,

1 cup sugar

Add, and stir until smooth,

½ cup water

Pour mixture, which should be like corn syrup, into 1-quart ring mold. Rotate to coat bottom and lower sides. Let it set. Beat together, until blended but not foamy,

4 whole eggs
4 egg yolks
⅓ cup sugar
⅛ teaspoon salt

Scald

1 cup heavy cream
2½ cups milk
1 inch scraped vanilla bean

Add to egg mixture. You may strain the mixture. Then pour, a little at a time, into prepared ring mold. Set mold in pan of boiling water and bake at 325° for 45 minutes. Remove and set in cold water to cool quickly. Chill. When ready to serve, unmold by running knife around inner and outer rims of mold. Unmold on serving plate and let stand a few minutes to allow syrup to run down over custard. Shake gently and lift off mold.

COLD PEACH SOUFFLÉ   *serves 6 to 8*

#1
Beat until lemon-colored

4 egg yolks
¾ cup sugar

Add

> 1 cup peach pulp from fresh or frozen, well-drained peaches
> 2 tablespoons lemon juice
> ½ cup dry white wine
> 1 tablespoon peach brandy

Cook in top of double boiler until mixture thickens. Soften

> 2 envelopes unflavored gelatin

in

> ½ cup cold water

Add to hot peach mixture, stirring until dissolved. Turn mixture into large bowl and refrigerate until thoroughly cooled, but not jelled. Whip

> 1 cup heavy cream

and beat until stiff

> 4 egg whites

Fold the cream and whites into peach mixture and pour into 2-quart soufflé dish or cut glass serving bowl. Chill completely. Serve with following sauce:

Sauce:

Scald in top of double boiler

> 1¼ cups milk

Beat slightly

>   2 egg yolks

Stir in

>   ¼ cup sugar
>   2½ tablespoons flour

Add yolk mixture to scalded milk and cook in double boiler over hot water about 7 minutes, stirring until mixture thickens. Cool. Add

>   2 tablespoons peach brandy

Serve cold over soufflé.

COLD RHUBARB SOUFFLÉ   *serves 8*

#1
Combine in saucepan

>   1½ pounds fresh rhubarb, cut into 1-inch lengths
>   ½ cup apple juice

Bring to a boil, cover, and simmer until tender, about 10 minutes. Put mix in blender and blend until smooth. Return to saucepan and add

>   ¾ cup light brown sugar
>   ½ teaspoon cinnamon
>   1 envelope unflavored gelatin
>   3 egg yolks

Heat briefly, stirring constantly, until gelatin dissolves and mixture begins to thicken. Do not boil. Cool and chill. Then fold in

    3 egg whites, stiffly beaten
    10 ounces heavy cream, whipped

Pour into 2-quart soufflé dish and chill several hours until ready to serve.

COFFEE PARFAIT

serves 8 to 10

Soften at room temperature

    3 pints coffee ice cream

Fold into ice cream
    1 cup heavy cream, whipped
    3 tablespoons instant coffee powder

Use this mixture to fill 8 to 10 parfait glasses. Freeze until firm. Then make a hole down center of each parfait. Fill it with

    8 to 10 tablespoons coffee liqueur

Top with

    ½ cup heavy cream, whipped

Freeze.

FRUIT WITH CREAM

serves 6 to 8

Combine

    1 (1-pound) can pear halves, drained
    1 (15¼-ounce) can pineapple spears, drained
    1 box fresh strawberries

Whip

    ½ cup heavy cream

Fold whipped cream into

    ½ cup sour cream

Add

    kirsch to taste

Pour over fruits. Any fresh fruits may be substituted. The creams may be folded together a few hours before serving.

GINGER PEACHY FLAN

serves 8

#1
Flan:

Cream together

    ⅓ cup butter
    ¼ cup sugar

Add and beat in

    1 egg yolk

Then add and mix to make firm dough

    1 cup unsifted flour

Roll into ball and chill 1 hour. Press chilled dough over bottom and sides of 10-inch flan ring. Prick all over with fork. Cover bottom with wax paper and fill with uncooked rice or dried beans. Bake at 400° for 10 minutes; remove rice and wax paper and, after reducing heat to 350°, bake 10 minutes more.

Filling:

Combine

    ½ cup sugar
    2 tablespoons cornstarch
    1 teaspoon salt
    ½ teaspoon ginger

Blend smooth with

    3 cups milk

Cook, stirring, until boiling and thick. Remove from heat and add

    2 teaspoons vanilla

Pour into baked flan shell. Peel, halve, and remove stones from

    6 fresh peaches

Cut each half into 3 pieces. Arrange evenly over pudding. Sprinkle with

> 1 cup macaroon crumbs

Bake 15 to 20 minutes at 400°. Chill.

GRAPE BAVARIAN

serves 6 to 8

#2
Dissolve

> 1 (3-ounce) package lemon-flavored gelatin

in

> 1 cup boiling water

Add

> 1 cup bottled grape juice

Chill until slightly thickened. Blend in

> 1 cup heavy cream, whipped

Spoon into 1-quart mold. Chill until firm. Garnish with additional whipped cream, if desired.

JELLIED MELON   *serves 8*

#2
Refreshing dessert.

Cut in half

    1 large ripe honeydew melon

Scoop balls from pulp and reserve shells. Fill shells with melon balls combined with

    ½ pint blueberries
    2 pears, peeled and diced
    ½ pound pitted cherries

Dissolve

    1 (3-ounce) package raspberry gelatin

in

    1½ cups boiling water

Cool, and pour over fruit in melon shells. Refrigerate to set. Cut into slices and serve on green leaves.

MACADAMIA NUT ICE BOX CAKE   *serves 8 to 10*

#1
Soften

> 1 envelope unflavored gelatin

in

> ¼ cup cold water

Place over simmering water and stir until dissolved. Remove from heat, but leave in water to keep warm. Beat

> 4 egg yolks

Beat in

> pinch of salt
> ¼ cup sugar

Gradually stir in

> 2 cups scalded milk

Cook over low heat, stirring constantly until mixture coats spoon. Add

> ½ teaspoon vanilla

and gelatin and cool to room temperature, stirring occasionally to prevent setting. Whip until stiff

> 1 cup heavy cream

Gradually add

¼ **cup sugar**

Add to custard mixture all but 2 tablespoons from

1 **(3½-ounce) jar macadamia nuts, finely chopped**

Fold in

cream

Line a 10-inch spring form pan, sides and bottom with

14 **whole lady fingers, split**

Pour in mixture and chill until set. Just before serving, whip

½ **cup heavy cream**

Gradually add

2 **tablespoons sugar**

Spread over custard mixture and decorate with

2 **tablespoons reserved nuts**

MARQUISE DE CHOCOLAT   *serves 8*

#1
Calorie watchers beware.

Melt in top of double boiler

8 **ounces semi-sweet chocolate**
½ **pound sweet butter**
3 **tablespoons superfine (instant) sugar**

Beat until light

6 egg yolks

Add the chocolate mixture gradually and beat at high speed for 10 minutes. Beat until stiff

6 egg whites

Add to whites

1 tablespoon superfine sugar
2 tablespoons coffee liqueur

Add to yolk mixture and beat at high speed for 10 minutes more. Pour into sherbet glasses. Refrigerate until ready to serve. Top with

dollop of whipped cream

PÊCHES FRANÇAISES   *serves 8*

#2
In a greased 9-by-13-inch pyrex baking dish, place

16 fresh peach halves

Fill the cavities of the peaches with

1 cup slivered almonds

Spoon over the peaches

½ cup orange liqueur
½ cup peach nectar

Bake at 250° for 2 hours, basting frequently. Serve the peaches chilled topped with

whipped cream or ice cream

RASPBERRY MACAROON MOUSSE

serves 8

✿

Puree in blender

2 (10-ounce) boxes frozen raspberries, thawed

Strain and pour into mixing bowl. Whip until stiff

2 cups heavy cream

Fold cream into raspberries. Beat until stiff

2 egg whites

Gradually beat in

½ cup sugar

Fold egg whites into cream mixture. Spoon into 1½-quart mold and freeze for 1 hour. Cover mousse with

⅔ cup crisp macaroon crumbs

Swirl with knife to form streaks. Freeze until firm. Place in refrigerator 2 hours before serving. Unmold and serve.

SHERLEY'S MOCHA ICE BOX CAKE *serves 12*

#1
Sherley Koteen has supplied recipes for every book we have written.

In top of double boiler melt

   2 (10-ounce) packages marshmallows
   1 cup strong black coffee
   ½ ounce unsweetened chocolate
   ¼ teaspoon salt

Cool thoroughly. Whip

   1½ pints heavy cream

Fold into marshmallow mixture with

   ½ cup finely chopped nuts

From a total of

   32 lady fingers

line the sides of a 10- or 12-inch spring form pan with whole lady fingers. Line the bottom of the spring form with split lady fingers. Pour ½ mousse mixture into prepared spring form. Cover

with split lady fingers and pour in remainder of mousse mixture.
Sprinkle top with

>   2 tablespoons chopped nuts

Chill overnight. Remove sides of spring form to serve.

STRAWBERRIES ROMANOFF   *serves 8 to 10*

Whip slightly

>   1 pint vanilla ice cream

Fold into it

>   ½ pint heavy cream, whipped

Add

>   juice of 1 lemon
>   2 ounces orange liqueur
>   1 ounce light rum

This may be prepared up to 2 hours ahead. When ready to serve,
pour sauce over

>   2 pints whole strawberries, sugared and chilled

Note: You may also use sauce over combination of berries such
as strawberries or raspberries and blueberries or over peaches or
cantaloupe balls and berries. Carry sauce to picnic in separate
covered plastic jar in insulated container to keep cold. Toss with
fruit when ready to serve.

STRAWBERRY NUT TART
serves 6 to 8

Beat together

> 5 egg yolks
> 1 cup sugar

Mix together

> 10 graham crackers rolled fine (1 cup crumbs)
> ¾ cup finely grated walnuts
> 1 teaspoon baking powder

Combine yolk mixture with cracker mixture. Fold in

> 5 egg whites, beaten stiff
> 1 teaspoon vanilla

Spoon into buttered 8-inch spring form pan and bake at 325° for 1 hour. Cool. When cool, spread top of tart with

> ½ cup strawberry jam

Sprinkle with

> 10 almond macaroons, crumbled

Refrigerate. To serve, spread with layer of

> ½ cup heavy cream, whipped

Top with

> ½ pint strawberries, crushed and sweetened with sugar

Drinks

ICED RUSSIAN CHOCOLATE

Into each tall glass, put

    2 to 3 tablespoons chocolate syrup
    1 ice cube

Fill glass with

    hot strong coffee
    scoop of chocolate ice cream

Top with

1 teaspoon whipped cream

ICED TEA

serves 8 to 10

This is an unusual method for making iced tea, eliminating the problem of a clouded brew which results when regularly brewed tea is refrigerated.

Fill a 2-quart jar with

8 cups cold water

Add

12 tea bags

Cover and chill in refrigerator 12 to 18 hours or overnight. Remove tea bags and pour tea into tall glasses filled with ice cubes. Serve with fresh mint sprigs, lemon and lime wedges, and sugar to taste.

ICED COFFEE

The quick method for making iced coffee is to prepare it double strength and pour it over ice cubes. In other words, for each measure of water in the coffee maker, use *two* standard coffee measures of ground beans. Then pour it, while hot, over the cubes.

NOTES AND HINTS ON LEFTOVER
TEA AND COFFEE

Do not refrigerate or beverage will become cloudy. Leftovers can be poured into ice cube trays and frozen. They are excellent for iced tea or coffee; when they are used, it is not necessary to make the beverage double strength. The melting cubes will simply add more liquid coffee.

After the cubes have frozen, they can be stored in plastic bags.

SANGRIA   *serves 8*

#1
From Americans living in Madrid.

Drain, reserving liquid, and dice

    1 (1-pound 4-ounce) can fruits for salad

Marinate fruits in mixture of reserved syrup and

    2 jiggers orange liqueur
    1 jigger brandy

When ready to serve, combine fruits and their marinade with

    1 quart Tom Collins carbonated soda
    1 bottle dry red wine
    lots of ice

Garnish with

lemon slices
orange slices
whole fresh strawberries

Serve in tall glasses.

SHANDY GAFF

The original Shandy Gaff was a bottle of ginger beer mixed with a pint of ale, or so one source indicates. But another calls for beer and ginger ale.

A modern version, invented by a friend from the beach, calls for beer and lemon and lime carbonated drink, in equal proportions.

We've gone one step further and made it with beer and dietetic lemon and lime carbonated beverage, equal parts. It's kind of like not having sugar in the coffee so you can eat the dessert. But it's delicious and very refreshing.

Index

Almond Crunch Rice, 114
Anita's Coffeecake, 163
Antipasto, Vegetable, 148
Appetizer Cheese Cake, 28
Applesauce Shortcake Squares, 184
Apricot Marzipan Tart, 164
Apricot Mold, Spiced, 144
Arabic or Syrian Bread, 152
Armenian Salad, 125
Avocado
  and Egg Salad, 132
  and Melon with Prosciutto, 41
  and Melon Salad, 126
  Zippy Dip, 52

Bacon-Wrapped Shrimp, 19
Bananas on the Grill, 106
Barbecued Beef Roast, 64
Barbecued Lamb with Plum Sauce, 65
Beans
  Dilly, 131
  Green, Marinated, 136
Bea's Ratatouille, 107
Beef and Barley Soup, 54
Beef Roast, Barbecued, 64
Beef Roll, Pic-L-Nic, 78
Betsy's Herb Bread, 153
Black Olives with Green Butter, 29
Blossie's Special, 196
Blue Cheese and Orange Salad, 138
Blueberry Pie with Orange Nut Crust, 166

Breads, 152–162
  Arabic or Syrian, 152
  Betsy's Herb, 153
  Cheese Buttermilk, 154
  Farmhouse, 155
  French, 156
  Herb, 157
  Onion Cheese, 159
  Onion Herb Ring, 160
  Orange Cranberry Muffins, 161
  Orange Pecan, 162
  Sticks, Herb, 157
  Yorkshire Puddings, Individual, 158
Broccoli
  Curried Chicken and, 88
  Flowers, 127
  Vinaigrette, 128
Brownie Torte, 167
Brownies, Three D, 194
Buttermilk-Cheese Bread, 154

Cabbage, Red, Filled with Cole Slaw, 140
Cakes
  Anita's Coffeecake, 163
  Apricot Marzipan Tart, 164
  Brownie Torte, 167
  Cheese Cake, Appetizer, 28
  Chocolate Nut Loaves, 168
  Devil's Food, 170
  Dundee, 171
  Glazed Chocolate Chip, 172
  Kataifi, 175
  Lemon Cream Torte, 176
  Peachy Cocoa Torte, 177

Praline, 178
Spicy Sponge, 181
Tipsy Delight, 182
See also Cold Desserts; Cookies
and Small Cakes
Calypso Chicken Barbecue, 84
Camembert Nut Sandwiches, 30
Caramel Flan, 197
Casserole, Chinese Rice, 116
Caviar
Eggplant, 39
-Frosted Cheese Mold, 31
Celery with Cheese Filling, 32
Cheese
Ball, Nippy Four, 43
Bars, Delice, 185
Buttermilk Bread, 154
Cake, Appetizer, 28
Chili, Roll, 35
Double, Roll, 38
Filling, Celery with, 32
Mold, Caviar Frosted, 31
Moon, 43
Pie, Italian, 174
Ring Loaf, 154
Cheese Taster's Choice, 32
Chicken
Barbecue, Calypso, 84
Curried, and Broccoli, 88
Farmer in the Dell, 90
Gauguin, 86
Grilled Lime, 91
Picnic Fried, 93
Pineapple Salad, 87
Provençal, Ernie's, 89
and Rice Salad, Nancy's, 92
Sesame, 94
in Tuna Sauce, 86
Wente, 95
Wings, Chinese, 20
Chicken Pâté Loaf, 33
Chick-Pea Salad, 129
Chili Cheese Roll, 35
Chili Con Sausage, 66
Chili Dip, 36
Chinese Chicken Wings, 20
Chinese Rice Casserole, 116

Chocolate Chip Cake, Glazed,
172
Chocolate Nut Loaves, 168
Chocoroon Cupcakes, Pat's, 193
Chowder, Rehoboth Beach, 60
Chutnut Roll, 37
Cocoa Torte, Peachy, 177
Coffee, Iced, 214
Coffee Parfait, 201
Coffee and Tea Leftover Hints,
215
Coffeecake, Anita's, 163
Cold Desserts, 196–212
Blossie's Special, 196
Caramel Flan, 197
Coffee Parfait, 201
Fruit with Cream, 202
Ginger Peachy Flan, 202
Grape Bavarian, 204
Jellied Melon, 205
Macadamia Nut Ice Box Cake,
206
Marquise de Chocolat, 207
Peach Soufflé, 198
Pêches Françaises, 208
Raspberry Macaroon Mousse,
209
Rhubarb Soufflé, 200
Sherley's Mocha Ice Box Cake,
210
Strawberries Romanoff, 211
Strawberry Nut Tart, 212
Cold Vegetables, *see* Salads and
Cold Vegetables
Cole Slaw, Red Cabbage Filled
with, 140
Cole Slaw Salad, 129
Confetti Rice, 117
Cookies and Small Cakes, 184–195
Applesauce Shortcake Squares,
184
Delice Cheese Bars, 185
Filled Marzipan Cookies, 187
Hello Dollys, 188
Lemon Curd Tarts, 188
Meringue Cookies, 189
Molasses Chewies, 190

Oatmeal Wafers, 191
Orange Marmalade Bars, 191
Pat's Chocoroon Cupcakes, 193
Pecan Tarts, 193
Three D Brownies, 194
Corn on the Cob, Roasted, 112
Corned Beef, Baked, 63
Crab Caper Dip, 37
Crabcakes, Maryland, 101
Crabmeat Surprise, 38
Cranberry Orange Muffins, 161
Cranberry Strawberry Mold, 145
Cucumber Mousse, 130
Cucumber Soup, 56
Cupcakes, Pat's Chocoroon, 193
Curried Chicken and Broccoli, 88
Curried Rice, 118
Curry, Lamb, 69
Curry Soup, Iced, 59

Danish Loaf, 98
Delice Cheese Bars, 185
Desserts, Cold, see Cold Desserts
Deviled Meat Balls, 21
Devil's Food Cake, 170
Dilly Beans, 131
Dips
  Chili, 36
  Crab Caper, 37
  Polynesian, 48
  Shangri La, 49
  Zippy Avocado, 52
Drinks, 213–216
  Iced Coffee, 214
  Iced Russian Chocolate, 213
  Iced Tea, 214
  Leftover Tea and Coffee Hints, 215
  Sangria, 215
  Shandy Gaff, 216
Dundee Cake, 171

Egg and Avocado Salad, 132
Eggplant Caviar, 39
Eggs, Stuffed, 50

Elkridge Tomatoes, 109
Empanadas, 22
Ernie's Chicken Provençal, 89

Farmer in the Dell, 90
Farmhouse Bread, 155
Flan
  Caramel, 197
  Ginger Peachy, 202
French Bread, 156
French Picnic Sandwich (Pain Bagnat), 102
Fruit with Cream, 202

Gauguin Chicken, 86
Gazpacho, 57
  Jiffy, 58
Ginger Peachy Flan, 202
Grape Bavarian, 204
Greek Salad, 132
Green Beans, Marinated, 136
Green Onion Pie, 110
Guacamole, 133
  Salad, 134
  Tomatoes, 135

Ham Pineapple Puffs, 23
Hamburgers Diable, 68
Hello Dollys, 188
Herb Bread, 157
Herb Bread, Betsy's, 153
Herb Sticks, 157
Honey Glazed Spareribs, 68
Honey Lime Salad, 135
Hors d'Oeuvres, Cold, 28–53
  Appetizer Cheese Cake, 28
  Black Olives with Green Butter, 29
  Camembert Nut Sandwiches, 30
  Caviar Frosted Cheese Mold, 31
  Celery with Cheese Filling, 32
  Cheese Taster's Choice, 32
  Chicken Pâté Loaf, 33
  Chili Cheese Roll, 35

Chili Dip, 36
Chutnut Roll, 37
Crab Caper Dip, 37
Crabmeat Surprise, 38
Double Cheese Roll, 38
Eggplant Caviar, 39
Italian Olive Spread, 40
Lulu Paste, 41
Melon and Avocado with Pro-
    sciutto, 41
Mock Pâté, 42
Moon Cheese, 43
Nippy Four Cheese Ball, 43
Parmesan Sticks, 45
Pâté en Terrine, 46
Pimiento Cheese Spread, 47
Polynesian Dip, 48
Potted Cheddar, 48
Shangri La Dip, 49
Shrimp Italiano, 49
Spiked Melon Balls, 50
Stuffed Eggs, 50
Stuffed Lychees, 51
Tom Thumbs, 52
Zippy Avocado Dip, 52
Hors d'Oeuvres, Hot, 19–27
    Bacon-Wrapped Shrimp, 19
    Chinese Chicken Wings, 20
    Deviled Meat Balls, 21
    Empanadas, 22
    Ham Pineapple Puffs, 23
    Olive Tarts, 24
    Pâté Quiche, 25
    Swiss Onion Pie, 26

Ice Box Cake
    Macadamia Nut, 206
    Sherley's Mocha, 210
Italian Cheese Pie, 174
Italian Olive Spread, 40
Italiano Shrimp, 49

Jellied Melon, 205
Jiffy Gazpacho, 58

Kataifi, 175

Lamb
    Barbecued with Plum Sauce, 65
    Curry, 69
    South African Shish Kebob, 81
    Southwestern, 82
Leftover Hints, Tea and Coffee,
    215
Lemon Cream Torte, 176
Lemon Curd Tarts, 188
Lemon Zucchini, 111
Lime Honey Salad, 135
Lobster Luncheon Salad, 100
London Broil Béarnaise, 71
Lulu Paste, 41
Lychees, Stuffed, 51

Macadamia Nut Ice Box Cake,
    206
Macaroni Picnic Bowl, 120
Macaroon Raspberry Mousse,
    209
Marmalade Bars, Orange, 191
Marquise de Chocolat, 207
Maryland Crabcakes, 101
Marzipan Cookies, Filled, 187
Meat Balls, Deviled, 21
Meat Dishes, 63–83
    Baked Corned Beef, 63
    Barbecued Beef Roast, 64
    Barbecued Lamb with Plum
        Sauce, 65
    Chili Con Sausage, 66
    Grilled Sirloin, 67
    Hamburgers Diable, 68
    Honey Glazed Spareribs, 68
    Lamb Curry, 69
    London Broil Béarnaise, 71
    Meat Loaf Lollipops, 72
    Michael's Steak, 73
    Moussaka à la Grecque, 74
    Norwegian Meat Pie, 76
    Picadinho, 77
    Pic-L-Nic Beef Roll, 78
    Poor Boy Sandwiches or Roman
        Grinders, 80
    Roast Beef Californian, 81

South African Shish Kebob, 81
Southwestern Lamb, 82
Melon
and Avocado with Prosciutto, 41
and Avocado Salad, 126
Balls, Spiked, 50
Jellied, 205
Menus, At Home, 7–13
Backyard Barbecue, 10, 12
Barbecue, 10, 11
Barbecue Feast, 13
Brunch (at home or away), 8
Cookout, 8
Curry Cookout, 10
Elegant Barbecue, 11
Family Reunion Barbecue, 12
International Barbecue, 12
Mexican Patio Fiesta, 8
One for the Kids-Cookout, 11
Patio, 7, 9
Patio Buffet, 9
Patio Dinner, 13
Patio Luncheon, 10
Patio Party for 8, 12
Rehoboth Patio Special, 9
Sunday Supper on Patio, 11
Menus, Picnic, 13–17
Barge Picnic, 14
Before the Concert, 13
Before the Summer Theater, 13
By the Side of a Stream, 17
Fête Champêtre, 15
French Countryside, 17
Greek Picnic, 17
Late Summer Mountain Lunch, 14
On the Beach, 14
On the Road, 15
Picnic to Carry Anywhere, 16
Picnic Luncheon at Stratford, 17
Picnic in the Park, 15
Sailing Picnic, 14
Store-bought Picnic, 16
Sunday School Picnic, 16
Tailgating—Night Game, 15

Meringue Cookies, 189
Michael's Steak, 73
Mocha Ice Box Cake, Sherley's, 210
Molasses Chewies, 190
Molded Salads
Cole Slaw Salad, 129
Cucumber Mousse, 130
Honey Lime, 135
Prize Winning Potato Salad, 139
Sea Breeze Spinach, 143
Spiced Apricot, 144
Strawberry Cranberry, 145
Moon Cheese, 43
Moussaka à la Grecque, 74
Mousse
Cucumber, 130
Raspberry Macaroon, 209
Muffins, Orange Cranberry, 161
Mushroom Caps, Stuffed, 146

Nancy's Chicken and Rice Salad, 92
Nippy Four Cheese Ball, 43
Noodle Pudding, Tene's, 124
Noodles Italienne, 121
Norwegian Meat Pie, 76
Nut Cake, Macadamia Ice Box, 205
Nut Loaves, Chocolate, 168
Nut Sandwiches, Camembert, 30
Nut Tart, Strawberry, 212

Oatmeal Wafers, 191
Olive Spread, Italian, 40
Olive Tarts, 24
Olives, Black, with Green Butter, 29
Onion Cheese Bread, 159
Onion Herb Ring, 160
Onion Pie
Green, 110
Swiss, 26
Orange and Blue Cheese Salad, 138

Orange Cranberry Muffins, 161
Orange Marmalade Bars, 191
Orange Nut Crust, Blueberry Pie
    with, 166
Orange Pecan Bread, 162
Oriental Salmon Steaks, 101

Pain Bagnat (French Picnic
    Sandwich), 102
Parfait, Coffee, 201
Parmesan Sticks, 45
Pâtés
    Chicken Loaf, 33
    En Terrine, 46
    Mock, 42
    Quiche, 25
Pat's Chocoroon Cupcakes, 193
Peach Soufflé, Cold, 198
Peachy Cocoa Torte, 177
Pecan Tarts, 193
Pêches Françaises, 208
Picadinho, 77
Pic-L-Nic Beef Roll, 78
Picnic Fried Chicken, 93
Picnic Sandwich, French (Pain
    Bagnat), 102
Pies
    Blueberry, with Orange Nut
        Crust, 166
    Green Onion, 110
    Italian Cheese, 174
    Norwegian Meat, 76
    Rhubarb and Strawberry, 180
    Swiss Onion, 26
Pimiento Cheese Spread, 47
Pineapple Chicken Salad, 87
Pineapple Ham Puffs, 23
Plum Sauce, Barbecued Lamb
    with, 65
Polynesian Dip, 48
Poor Boy Sandwiches or Roman
    Grinders, 80
Potato, Noodle, and Rice Dishes,
    114–124
    Almond Crunch Rice, 114
    Baked Potatoes Florentine,
    115

Chinese Rice Casserole, 116
Confetti Rice, 117
Curried Rice, 118
Hot Potato Salad, 119
Macaroni Picnic Bowl, 120
Noodles Italienne, 121
Potatoes in Armor, 122
Sunshine Pasta, 123
Tene's Noodle Pudding, 124
Potato Salads
    Hot, 119
    Molded Prize Winning, 139
Potted Cheddar, 48
Poultry Dishes, 84
    Calypso Chicken Barbecue, 84
    Chicken Gauguin, 86
    Chicken Pineapple Salad, 87
    Chicken in Tuna Sauce, 86
    Curried Chicken and Broccoli,
        88
    Ernie's Chicken Provençal, 89
    Farmer in the Dell, 90
    Grilled Lime Chicken, 91
    Nancy's Chicken and Rice
        Salad, 92
    Picnic Fried Chicken, 93
    Sesame Chicken, 94
    Wente Chicken, 95
Praline Cake, 178

Quiche Pâté, 25

Raspberry Macaroon Mousse,
    209
Ratatouille, Bea's, 107
Red Cabbage Filled with Cole
    Slaw, 140
Red Snapper with Tomato Sauce,
    103
Rehoboth Beach Chowder, 60
Rhubarb Soufflé, Cold, 200
Rhubarb and Strawberry Pie,
    180
Rice
    Almond Crunch, 114
    Casserole, Chinese, 116

and Chicken Salad, Nancy's, 92
Confetti, 117
Curried, 118
Roast Beef Californian, 81
Roman Grinders or Poor Boy Sandwiches, 80
Roman Salad, 141
Russian Chocolate, Iced, 213

Salade Niçoise, 142
Salads and Cold Vegetables, 125–151
Armenian Salad, 125
Avocado and Melon Salad, 126
Broccoli Flowers, 127
Broccoli Vinaigrette, 128
Chicken Pineapple Salad, 87
Chicken and Rice Salad, Nancy's, 92
Chick-Pea Salad, 129
Cole Slaw, 129
Cucumber Mousse, 130
Dilly Beans, 131
Egg and Avocado Salad, 132
Greek Salad, 132
Guacamole, 133
Guacamole Salad, 134
Guacamole Tomatoes, 135
Honey Lime Salad, 135
Lobster Luncheon Salad, 100
Marinated Green Beans, 136
Mixed Bag Salad, 137
Mixed Vegetable Salad, 138
Orange and Blue Cheese Salad, 138
Potato Salad, Hot, 119
Prize Winning Molded Potato Salad, 139
Red Cabbage Filled with Cole Slaw, 140
Roman Salad, 141
Salade Niçoise, 142
Sea Breeze Spinach Mold, 143
Spiced Apricot Mold, 144

Strawberry Cranberry Mold, 145
Stuffed Mushroom Caps, 146
Three Bean Salad, 146
Tomato Cheese Salad, 147
Vegetable Antipasto, 148
Vegetable Salad, 148
Western Toss, 150
Zucchini Salad, 150
Salmon-Sauce Verte, Cold, 97
Salmon Steaks, Oriental, 101
Sandwiches
Camembert Nut, 30
French Picnic (Pain Bagnat), 102
Poor Boy or Roman Grinders, 80
Sangria, 215
Saumon en Croute, 104
Sausage, Chili Con, 66
Sea Breeze Spinach Mold, 143
Seafood Dishes, 97
Cold Salmon—Sauce Verte, 97
Danish Loaf, 98
Lobster Luncheon Salad, 100
Maryland Crabcakes, 101
Oriental Salmon Steaks, 101
Pain Bagnat (French Picnic Sandwich), 102
Red Snapper with Tomato Sauce, 103
Saumon en Croute, 104
Sesame Chicken, 94
Shandy Gaff, 216
Shangri La Dip, 49
Sherley's Mocha Ice Box Cake, 210
Shish Kebob, South African, 81
Shortcake Squares, Applesauce, 184
Shrimp, Bacon Wrapped, 19
Shrimp Bisque, Chilled, 55
Shrimp Italiano, 49
Sirloin, Grilled, 67
Small Cakes, see Cookies and Small Cakes

Soufflé, Cold
    Peach, 198
    Rhubarb, 200
Soups, 54–62
    Beef and Barley, 54
    Chilled Shrimp Bisque, 55
    Cucumber, 56
    Easy Vichyssoise, 57
    Gazpacho, 57
    Iced Curry, 59
    Jiffy Gazpacho, 58
    Rehoboth Beach Chowder, 60
    Spinach, 61
    Tomato Lime, 62
South African Shish Kebob, 81
Southwestern Lamb, 82
Spareribs, Honey Glazed, 68
Spinach Mold, Sea Breeze, 143
Spinach Soup, 61
Steaks
    Grilled Sirloin, 67
    Michael's, 73
    Salmon, Oriental, 101
Strawberries Romanoff, 211
Strawberry Cranberry Mold, 145
Strawberry Nut Tart, 212
Strawberry and Rhubarb Pie, 180
Sunshine Pasta, 123
Swiss Onion Pie, 26
Syrian or Arabic Bread, 152

Tarts
    Apricot Marzipan, 164
    Lemon Curd, 188
    Olive, 24
    Pecan, 193
    Strawberry Nut, 212
Tea, Iced, 214
Tea and Coffee Leftover Hints, 215
Tene's Noodle Pudding, 124

Three Bean Salad, 146
Three D Brownies, 194
Tipsy Delight, 182
Tom Thumbs, 52
Tomato Cheese Salad, 147
Tomato Lime Soup, 62
Tomatoes
    Broiled Seasoned, 108
    Elkridge, 109
    Guacamole, 135
Torte
    Brownie, 167
    Lemon Cream, 176
    Peachy Cocoa, 177
Tuna Sauce, Chicken in, 86

Vegetable Antipasto, 148
Vegetable Salad, 148
Vegetables, 106–113
    Bananas on the Grill, 106
    Bea's Ratatouille, 107
    Broiled Seasoned Tomatoes, 108
    Elkridge Tomatoes, 109
    Green Onion Pie, 110
    Lemon Zucchini, 111
    Roasted Corn on the Cob, 112
    Zucchini with Sour Cream, 113
    See also Salads and Cold Vegetables
Vichyssoise, Easy, 57

Wafers, Oatmeal, 191
Wente Chicken, 95
Western Toss, 150

Yorkshire Puddings, Individual, 158

Zucchini, Lemon, 111
Zucchini Salad, 150
Zucchini with Sour Cream, 113